On the Death of Childhood and the Destruction of Public Schools

The Folly of Today's Education Policies and Practices

Gerald W. Bracey

D1550609

HEINEMANN ■ Portsmouth, NH

Heinemann
A division of Reed Elsevier Inc.
361 Hanover Street
Portsmouth, NH 03801–3912
www.heinemann.com

Offices and agents throughout the world

The author and publisher wish to thank those who have generously given permission to reprint borrowed material:

"Failing Children—Twice," "The Malevolent Tyranny of Algebra," "International Comparisons: An Excuse to Avoid Meaningful Educational Reform," and "The Right's Data-Proof Ideologues" originally appeared in *Education Week*. Copyright by Gerald W. Bracey.

"School Should *Not* Prepare Students for the World of Work" first appeared in the *NASSP Bulletin*, September 1996. Reprinted by permission of NASSP.

"April Foolishness: 'A Nation At Risk' at Twenty" first appeared in *Phi Delta Kappan*, April 2003. Reprinted by permission of Phi Delta Kappan.

"Getting Dumber in School?" first appeared in *Principal Leadership*, March 2001. Reprinted by permission of NASSP.

"Playing It Crooked: Media and Political Distortion About the Condition of American Public Schools" is reprinted from *Best Practices, Best Thinking, and Emerging Issues in School Leadership* by Gerald W. Bracey. Reprinted by permission of Sage Publications, Inc.

"Long-Term Studies of Preschool: The Benefits Far Outweigh the Costs" first appeared in *Phi Delta Kappan*, June 2003. Reprinted by permission of Phi Delta Kappan.

Library of Congress Cataloging-in-Publication Data
Bracey, Gerald W. (Gerald Watkins)
    On the death of childhood and the destruction of public schools : the folly of today's education policies and practices / Gerald W. Bracey.
        p. cm.
    Includes bibliographical references.
    ISBN 0-325-00602-4 (alk. paper)
        1. Public schools—United States. 2. Education and state—United States.
3. Education—United States—Evaluation.   I. Title.

LA217.2.B725 2003
371.01'0973—dc21   2003011650

Editor: Lois Bridges
Production service: Colophon
Production coordination: Vicki Kasabian
Cover design: Night and Day Design
Typesetter: Tom Allen, Pear Graphic Design
Manufacturing: Steve Bernier

Printed in the United States of America on acid-free paper
07   06   05   04   03   VP   1   2   3   4   5

ontents

Acknowledgments

Working out of one's home makes one more independent than when one occupies a normal position in some institution peopled with other human beings. Still, there are others involved. In this case my unofficial (and very sharp) editors—my wife, Iris, and my mother-in-law, Teddie Berket. They also tolerated my hermit-like existence in the basement with great patience, even when they were on the first floor, yearning to eat dinner. Such tolerance was also shown, on some occasions, by Raki, our reigning cairn terrier who really, really wanted me to take him to the marina park where he could indulge his passion for chasing squirrels. I would also like to acknowledge Heinemann editor Lois Bridges, whose enthusiasm and help made this book possible.

$\mathscr{I}$ntroduction
The Voyage to Contrarianism

I didn't set out to become a contrarian, although I think I must have had natural leanings that way. Even before I embarked, one friend had once called me a "professional outsider," and another told me, "You've made a career out of asking, 'How do you know that?'" I have done that and I am constantly amazed that the knowledge base people offer as their warrant for strong, sometimes outrageous assertions is so weak, incomplete, and, too often, erroneous.

Still, at the time my journey toward refuting the conventional wisdom about public schools began, I didn't even notice. I was comfortably installed in a conventional job in a conventional institution: Director of Research and Evaluation for the Cherry Creek, Colorado, school district. The job kept my days full and, like my colleagues, I didn't really have much spare time to reflect on, much less verify, whether all the terrible things we heard about the nation's public schools were really true.

But, though I didn't know it then, my life changed over morning coffee on November 5, 1990. That day, the *Denver Post* reprinted "Johnny's Miserable SATs," a column by *Washington Post* pundit Richard Cohen.[1] Cohen's column caused me to conduct my own analysis of SAT trends, taking into account the vast demographic changes in who takes the SAT. (The SAT standards were set on 10,654 white kids living in New England. Almost half had attended private, college prep high schools.) I reached quite different conclusions than Cohen, conclusions that *Education Week* carried under the title, "SAT Scores: Miserable or Miraculous?"[2] My life would never be the same.

As it happened, a group of engineers at Sandia National Laboratories that had conducted a large study of schools also concluded that American public schools were performing much better than the critics claimed. After they saw my essay, some of them came up from Albuquerque to Denver and we shared our data (I had more than SAT scores by then). The first Bush administration, trying to push vouchers and tuition tax credits, suppressed their report, but they gave me the data and told me to run with it.[3] I did.

I ran to *Phi Delta Kappan* with an article, "Why Can't They Be Like We Were?," which appeared in the October 1991 issue. At the time, I thought I had presented sufficient data from a sufficiently wide variety of sources to have proven that the schools were doing better than critics claimed. Some indicators even stood at record highs. I thought that would be the end of it—I wouldn't have to write anything else. Pauline Gough, the editor of *Kappan* at the time, thought so too. I recall her saying, "I guess they can't say nasty things about the schools anymore." Boy, were we naïve.

In early 1992, much more data came to my attention and I sent a follow-up article to *Kappan* with the title, "The True Crisis in Public Education," and a Post-It note on the first page. It expressed my dissatisfaction with the title and asked the editors to compose something more attention grabbing, something "more zippy" was the way I put it. Their zippy title was "The Second Bracey Report on the Condition of Public Education," and they asked that it be an annual event. The Thirteenth Bracey Report appears in October 2003.

My willingness to go against the grain, to attack the conventional wisdom, earned me favor in some quarters and disdain in others. (In spring 2003, George Mason University, where I have a part-time position, invited former assistant secretary of education Chester E. Finn, Jr., to speak to the faculty. When Finn realized that I was on the faculty, he said he would not speak if I were in the room.) But every time I turned around, it seemed I was finding some additional data that bolstered my contention.

In addition to my annual reports, over the years I generated a number of mostly shorter essays on single topics and issues. Some of these got published, mostly in education periodicals such as *Education Week* and the publications of various professional education organizations. A few made it to *USA Today* and the *Washington Post,* but while the public rates education as an important issue, most op-ed pages do not and many of the essays languished on my hard drive.

A little more than half of this collection has seen print somewhere else. Almost all of these essays have been modified slightly to bring them up to date or to introduce additional relevant material that, although relevant, would have made the essays too long for the 750-word limits on op-ed submissions.

The reader will find an underlying tone of anger in some of the essays and overt anger in others. This should surprise no one. I think virtually all of the dominant reforms in the last twenty years have been wrongheaded. (I choose a period of twenty years ago because that marked the appearance of a golden treasury of selected, spun, and distorted statistics, "A Nation At Risk.") I was an early supporter of standards. I thought they could be useful in the same way as having major league baseball teams and virtuoso instrument players can be instructive to little league ballplayers and music students, respectively. But, as is so often the case in education reform, the standards movement soon turned ugly and punitive, especially when coupled with what became a juggernaut—high-stakes testing. (The idea that education can or should be enjoyable has never garnered much favor from the general public, and politicians have found that they can get elected more easily if they promise to "get tough" with the schools.)

Worse than misguided reforms are the overt attempts to destroy the public schools system (among the lessons learned in the last decade: Good news about public schools serves no one's education reform agenda). These I have chronicled in *The War against America's Public Schools* and *What You Should Know about the War against America's Public Schools*. A few pieces, such as "Edison's Light Dims: The Rise and Fall and Rise and Fall of H. Christopher Whittle" and "The No Child Left Behind Act, a Plan for the Destruction of Public Education: Just Say No," also deal with this war.

At this moment, the war against Iraq is mostly over, and the war on public schools continues unabated. Both Colorado and Louisiana considered voucher bills this year, Colorado passing a voucher law, Louisiana defeating the bill. On March 25, 2003, the Arizona Senate approved a bill to provide dollar-for-dollar tax credits for companies that contribute up to $100,000 for scholarships to private schools. The bill is worth $10 now and will grow annually by $10 million up to a limit of $50 million. The same day, the Florida House of Representatives passed a law granting corporations tax credits for up to $10 million a year for contributions to private school vouchers for use by the children of people in military service. The *St. Petersburg Times* wryly observed "When Democrats suggested the tax credit might be more fairly spent on encouraging civilian employers to maintain the pay of reservists called to active duty, Republican sponsors didn't pretend to have a good answer. Could that be because the bill is less about patriotism than about helping private schools and hurting the public schools?"[4]

One essay, "April Foolishness," debunks "A Nation At Risk" on its twentieth anniversary. Several take on the testing movement: "Testing Flunks Life," "The Governors' Debacle," "The Testing–Talent Disconnect," and "A Surefire Way to Destroy America: Test Every Kid Every Year."

One section offers data that provide different perspectives than usually seen. "What If 'Failing Schools' Aren't?" shows that poor kids gain as much during the school year as middle-class kids, but lose it over the summer. "Getting Dumber in School?" partly accepts and partly rejects the notion that American kids lose ground to their peers in other developed nation the longer they stay in school. "Those Misleading SAT and NAEP Trends" shows that the usual way these tests are reported obscures the very real gains that have been made on both. "The Dumbing of America?" provides a history of education reform and reveals that there never was a Golden Age of American public education. Reviewing the history of public schools, one sees them including more and more people and raising achievement at the same time.

The group of pieces under the heading Explaining the World takes on some of the current policy issues in education. "Playing It Crooked" looks at how the media distort the condition of schools—with a great deal of help from businessmen and politicians. "Long-Term Studies of Preschool" presents data to argue that investing in quality preschool pays off in the long run. "Horace Mann and Today's Mandates" attempts to enter the mind of the father of American public education to see what he might say about the nuttiness of today's policies.

On January 15, 2003, Herb Levine, the Superintendent of Schools in Salem, Massachusetts, said, "I really believe that 50 years from now, we will look upon those who support high-stakes testing requirements as we now look upon cavemen." I hope he's right in that that comes to pass, but I also hope he's wrong—I hope that we can shift that attitude much faster than two-and-a-half generations.

I can only hope that reading the essays in this volume will speed up the needed perspective transformation.

Notes

1. Richard Cohen, "Johnny's Miserable SATs." *Washington Post*, September 4, 1990, p. A19.

2. Gerald W. Bracey, "SAT Scores: Miserable or Miraculous?" *Education Week*, November 21, 1990.

3. The official story from assistant secretary of education Diane Ravitch was that the report contained errors and was not yet acceptable as a "professional" publication. Although compiled in 1990, the report never attained "professional" status and remained unpublished, although thousands of "underground" copies were circulated by me and others who had obtained it. In recent years, a now-retired vice president of Sandia who oversaw the compilation of the report advised me it was definitely suppressed. Once Ravitch and the others were deposed by the Clinton administration, the report could be aired. Although never published by the Department of Energy, which commissioned it, or the Department of Education, which suppressed it, it finally appeared in the May/June 1993 issue of the *Journal of Educational Research*.

4. *St. Petersburg Times*, "Patriotic Disguise." March 25, 2003.

The No Child Left Behind Act, a Plan for the Destruction of Public Education
Just Say No

The No Child Left Behind Act is a trap. It is the grand scheme of the school privatizers. No Child Left Behind (NCLB) sets up public schools for the final knock down.

Paranoia? Hardly. Consider that the Bush administration is deregulating every pollution-producing industry in sight while cutting Superfund cleanup money. It has rolled back regulations on power plants and snowmobiles and wants to take protection away from twenty million acres of wetlands (20 percent of the total). President Bush's response to global warming: "Deal with it!" by which he means adjust to it while we make the world safe for SUVs. The president wants to outsource hundreds of thousands of government jobs to private corporations.[1] He wants, in other words, to get the government out of government.

> *The No Child Left Behind Act is a trap. It is the grand scheme of the school privitizers.*

Would an administration with such an antiregulatory, proprivate sector policy perspective turn around and impose harsh, straitjacket requirements on schools, demands that would bankrupt any business? Of course not. Unless it had an ulterior purpose.

Recall that the president's original 2001 proposal provided

vouchers to let children attend private schools at taxpayer expense. Congress, chastised by the massive defeats vouchers suffered in referenda in California and Michigan in the 2000 election (voucher proponents outspent opponents 2–1, but the measures went down in flames, 70–30, in both states), stripped the voucher provisions from the bill. Congress didn't strip them from Karl Rove's mind. After the 2002 elections, the *Wall Street Journal* declared, "GOP's Election Gains Give School Vouchers a Second Wind."[2] They'll be back. In fact, they already are. President Bush has put $75 million for vouchers for the District of Columbia in his 2004 budget proposal, and some congressmen want to extend their use to other cities as well.[3]

There are any number of impossible-to-meet provisions in the NCLB, but let's take just two of the most prominent: those for testing and those for teacher qualifications. The federal government cannot force NCLB on states, but any state that wants NCLB money must agree to test all children in grades three through eight every year in reading and math and, two years later, science as well. The tests must be based on "challenging" standards, and schools must show "adequate yearly progress" (AYP) until, by 2014, all of the schools' students attain the "proficient" level. The school must demonstrate AYP overall and separately for all major ethnic and socioeconomic groups, special education students, and English Language Learners. And pigs will fly.

In his 2003 presidential address to the American Educational Research Association convention, Robert Linn revealed the ludicrousness of the AYP requirement. Linn, the co-director of the Center for the Study of Evaluation, Student Standards and Testing at UCLA and the University of Colorado showed with cold numbers how long it will take the country to attain the targets mandated by the No Child Left Behind Act (NCLB). If the nation makes the same progress on tests as it has made in the last decade, it will attain the required level of proficiency in fourth grade math in 2060, in eighth grade math in 2067, and in twelfth grade math in 2169. Conversely, if the nation is to reach the NCLB targets by the required date of 2014, it must accelerate improvement by a factor of 4 in grades four and eight and by a factor of 12 in grade twelve.

The massive testing requirements alone will force many states to spend massive amounts of money to develop, administer, analyze, and report the test results and other data needed for mandatory "report cards" schools must develop and send to parents. Many states will have to abandon their own programs labored over for the last decade—or two. Their costs may well exceed what NCLB provides. An analysis by Rutland, Vermont, School Superintendent William Mathis found that the state will receive $52 million dollars from NCLB, but that it will cost the Green Mountain State $158 million to implement the law's provisions.[4] Mathis estimates that national cost to states at between $84 billion and $148 billion.[5]

The word *proficient* is a trap, too. According to the law, each state decides how to define it, but the word already has great currency in education circles

> NCLB provided the states with $1.4 billion in new money. It will cost the states between $84 and $148 billion.

as part of the lingo surrounding the National Assessment of Educational Progress (NAEP). It is one of the NAEP achievement levels, the others being "below basic," "basic," and "advanced." Not many children attain the proficient level on NAEP tests.

Although in common parlance, the NAEP achievement levels have been rejected by everyone who has ever studied them: Linn's Center for Research on Evaluation, Student Standards and Testing (CRESST),[6] the General Accounting Office,[7] and the National Academy of Sciences,[8] as well as by individual psychometricians such as Lyle Jones of the University of North Carolina.[9] The studies agree that the methods used are flawed, confusing, internally inconsistent, and lack evidence of validity. Most important, the results don't accord with any other data.

For instance, Jones pointed out that American fourth graders were well above average on the mathematics tests of the Third International Mathematics and Science Study (TIMSS), yet only 18 percent reached the proficient level and a meager 2 percent scored at the advanced level in the 1996 NAEP mathematics. Similarly only 29 percent attained the proficient level in the 1996 NAEP Science assessment but in TIMSS Science, American fourth graders were third in the world among twenty-six nations. Finally, on the 2000 NAEP reading assessment, only 32 percent of fourth graders attained proficient or better, but American nine-year-olds were second in the world among twenty-seven countries in the international reading study, *How in the World Do Students Read?*[10,11] It makes no sense that American kids do so poorly on domestic measures such as NAEP but stack up well against the rest of the industrialized world. Oh, yes, theoretically the rest of the world's kids are dolts, too, but no one actually believes that.

The NAEP achievement levels were developed at a time when the National Assessment Governing Board was controlled by Chester E. Finn, Jr., and other ideologues on the Right. Their purpose was to sustain the sense of crisis created by 1983's golden treasury of selected, spun, and distorted statistics, "A Nation At Risk." NABG hired three of the most respected evaluators in the country to evaluate the NAEP standards and standard-setting process. When the evaluators reported that the process didn't work, NAGB summarily fired them. Or tried to. The contract forbade it.

When NAEP was first introduced, the enabling law forbade it to report at the state level. Congress revised the law in 1988 to make state reporting possible, and currently about forty states volunteer (and pay) to receive state-level information. Under NCLB, state-level NAEP goes from voluntary to mandatory. All states must participate in the biennial NAEP reading and math assessments to "confirm" their own results. Studies have already shown that a much smaller proportion of students reaches "proficient" on NAEP than on the various state tests. In Texas, for example, 91 percent of the students hit the proficient level on the state eighth grade math test, but only 24 percent managed to attain proficiency on NAEP eighth grade math. Because the NAEP levels are exceedingly high, Linn observed that even getting all children to even the "basic" level on NAEP would constitute a mighty challenge.[12]

The NCLB bill contains incentives for states to start at a low level (to have any prayer of achieving AYP). This is why, on a preliminary analysis of "failing schools" in various states, Michigan (with high standards) had 1,513 failing schools, and Arkansas (with low standards) had none. Yet on the fourth grade NAEP reading assessment in 2000, Michigan had 28 percent of its students at or above proficient, while Arkansas had only 23 percent. Differences like this will turn into discrepancies between what the state assessments say and what NAEP says about how many students in a state are or are not proficient. Critics and profit seekers will take the discrepancy between the state results and the NAEP results as evidence that the schools are *still* failing and that the states and districts are lying to their citizens about school quality.

Districts and schools that fail to make AYP are subject to increasingly severe—and unworkable—sanctions. Their staffs can be fired, their kids sent to another district, the district abolished.

Using the original formulation, the White House's own calculations revealed that had NCLB been in place for a few years, about 90 percent of the schools in North Carolina and Texas would have been labeled "failing schools." North Carolina and Texas? These are states that have been singled out in recent years for their progress on a variety of tests. If they can't meet the standards, what hope is there for the rest? None—that's the purpose of the law. The National Conference of State Legislatures estimated that 90 percent of all schools would fail, while simulations by the Council of Chief State School Officers put the failure rate at only 88 percent.[13] As a consequence, some wags are beginning to refer to the law as LNSS: Let No School Succeed. At the 2003 AERA convention, one long-time U.S. Department of Education employee told me the law should be renamed, not NCLB, but NCL-B.S.

In a move clearly aimed at greasing the skids for vouchers, the U.S. Department of Education put out regulations that make no sense at all. As a first step to quashing failing schools, children in those schools must be offered the option of going to a more successful one, *successful* defined solely in terms of test scores. It does not matter if the "successful" schools are already stuffed to the gills. They must hire more teachers (where they will find them is something of a mystery), bring in trailers, or build more classrooms (where they will get the money is something of a mystery). They must, in the words of Under Secretary Eugene Hickok, build capacity. Only if the arriving students would so crowd the schools as to violate fire or other safety and health codes, can they be denied access. Thus, in theory, we could face a situation in which virtually all students attend schools currently enrolling only 10 percent of students. In some places, one must truly wonder where kids will go. Los Angeles has enough classroom space for 145,000 high schoolers. The district currently has 165,000, with a projected 200,000 by 2005.[14]

There are more than a few technical problems with the concept of AYP. Researchers have found that test scores at the school level are quite volatile from year to year.[15] According to RAND researcher David Grissmer, the tests would not identify the good and the bad schools, but only the lucky and unlucky ones.[16] Not only are the test scores volatile, most of the volatility is associated with factors that have nothing to do with what goes on in the classroom.

No one has given any consideration to student mobility. Nationally, 20 percent of American students change schools each year. In urban areas the figure is more like 50 percent, and in some instances, the students in a building at the end of the year are not those who started there in the fall. How, then, can the *school* be considered failing or succeeding?

Similarly, nothing in the law takes into account the phenomenon of summer loss. This is critical. Disadvantaged students show substantial summer loss, while middle-class and affluent students hold their own in mathematics and actually gain over the summer months in reading. One study found that poor and middle-class students gained the same amount during the school year, but, because of summer losses, the poor students fell farther and farther behind their middle-class peers as they moved from first to fifth grade.[17] Thus, *schools* that actually make adequate yearly progress during the school year will get labeled as failures because of what happens during the summer months.

Moreover, no one has given any attention to what happens when large numbers of children leave "failing" schools for more successful ones. (The U.S. Department of Education has given large grants for publicity campaigns to ensure that parents are aware of this option.) Suppose the arriving students raise the average class size from twenty-two to twenty-nine students. This alone could easily transform a successful school into a failing one.

And what kinds of test scores will the arriving students bring? The legislation demands that schools give priority to the neediest students—those with the lowest test scores. The arrival of large numbers of low-scoring students might well convert a successful school into a failing one. At the same time, because the departing students take their low scores with them, the sending school's test scores will automatically rise. But if the sending school gets out of the failing category, it doesn't get the kids back. It only gets to stop paying for their transportation, thereby turning NCLB into an unfunded mandate on parents.

Students who leave a "failing" school automatically raise that school's test scores and lower the test scores of the receiving school.

The preceding problems present sufficient difficulties for schools, but their lives become more arduous because they must disaggregate the data below the school level. As mentioned, school-level test scores show volatility from year to year. Imagine what kind of instability we'll see when we have reports by smaller units: blacks, whites, Hispanics, Asians, Native Americans, special education students, kids on free and reduced-price lunches, and English Language Learners. And if one *group* doesn't show AYP, the *school* takes the hit.

When the preordained high failure rate occurs, vouchers and privatization will be touted as the only possible cures. Subsequent to the voucher defeats in Michigan and California, voucher advocates have stopped touting vouchers as a cure-all for the whole nation on market grounds and have started pushing them for poor people on civil rights grounds. They contend that middle class people aren't interested in vouchers, because they think their public schools are good (they're right). But with the high failure rates guaranteed by NCLB, even those good schools will fail—51 percent of the schools in North Carolina recognized for "exemplary growth" failed under NCLB.[18] Conservative school critic Denis Doyle wrote that the NCLB means that the nation is about to be "inundated in a sea of bad news" and that the schools are going to get "pole-axed."[19]

The privatizers will shout, "The school system has proven it is an ossified government monopoly that can't reform itself (Chester Finn shouted precisely this in 1998 in the *Wall Street Journal*[20]). You've had your chance. We warned you. We gave you 'Nation At Risk' over twenty years ago. Nothing has changed. It's time to apply American business expertise to education." Right, as in Enron, Tyco, Global Crossing, Imclone, WorldCom, the 993 companies that have "adjusted" their accounting reports in the last five years, and the myriad dot.coms that failed because their officers didn't have a clue about how to run a business. (How come no one ever criticizes *business* schools?)

If not yet in bankruptcy court, Chris Whittle and his Edison Schools Inc., will be waiting. (Edison stock has been as high as $39 a share, but in July 2003 it was hovering around $1.50; in ten years, the company has failed to show a profit in even one quarter.) Recall that Whittle announced his plan for a national system of private schools in 1991 when President George Herbert Walker

Bush was riding high after the Gulf War. So certain was a Bush reelection—coronation, actually—that the most likely Democratic candidates declined to run and left the certain defeat to the Governor of Arkansas.

Recall, too, that Whittle had paid Bush's secretary of Education, Lamar Alexander, $125,000 as a consultant while Alexander was Governor of Tennessee (Whittle Communications was headquartered in Knoxville). Alexander also bought $10,000 worth of Whittle Communications stock. He transferred the stock to his wife when he became president of the University of Tennessee (for some reason, his wife also wrote a check to Whittle for the shares). Apparently, Whittle never cashed either one of them, but he later bought the stock back for $330,000.[21]

Whittle's original grandiose plan prophesied two hundred private schools by 1996 and one thousand by 2000. (He currently manages, not owns, about 130 public schools.) He said it would require about $1 billion to create a prototype of his scheme and another $2 billion to ramp it up to a national scale. Where on earth would he get that kind of money? Whittle said from bankers and investors. Three billion from investors who had already lost about $400 million on his earlier adventure, Channel One? Whittle actually needed Bush and Alexander to push their school voucher plan through Congress. Then children could use those vouchers to attend Edison schools.

When the unthinkable happened and Bush lost, Whittle had to fall back on managing a few public schools. Whittle no doubt already has an advertising campaign ready for when the failing grades start arriving. He will then portray the Edison "model" as the only means of consistently achieving AYP, even though evaluations have found Edison achievement results mixed at best and a dozen schools that Edison lists as showing "positive" trends have terminated their contracts.

But Edison has friends in high places. Lamar Alexander is now a senator who managed, despite his freshman status, to wrangle a seat on the education committee. Another fan, Eugene Hickok, is Deputy Secretary of Education (Hickok was responsible for persuading then-Pennsylvania governor, Tom Ridge, to impose Edison on Philadelphia schools). And a third Whittle pal and voucher advocate, Lisa Keegan, heads the Education Leaders Council (in which Hickok was very active before taking his current appointment), which has received millions in no-bid contracts from Secretary of Education Rod Paige. Whittle will be ready to roll if the moment comes, as will be former secretary of education, William J. Bennett. Bennett now heads K12, Inc., funded by former junk bond king, Michael Milken's Knowledge Universe. After decades of warning people that computers offer no educational advantages, Bennett converted and is now gambling on a company that produces online curriculum materials. The "supplementary providers" provisions of NCLB offer Whittle, Bennett, and other private companies opportunities after the public schools "fail."

The testing requirements alone are enough to consign the schools to failure. The requirements for "highly qualified" teachers simply hit the schools while they're down. All current teachers in schools receiving NCLB funds must be "highly qualified" by 2005–2006, as must anyone who was hired after the 2002–2003 school year began. By "highly qualified," NCLB means those who hold at least a bachelor's degree, have full state certification (or have passed the state's licensing exam), and who have not had any certification requirements waived on "an emergency, provisional, or temporary basis."

There are nationwide shortages of people with such qualifications in mathematics, science, and special education. Shortages are particularly acute in the cities. Chicago says 25 percent of the teachers in low-performing schools don't meet the requirements,[22] while Baltimore puts the figure at 31 percent.[23] A 2003 survey commissioned by Education Week shows that 22 percent of all high school students take a course from a teacher without even a minor in the subject. For high-poverty high schools, the figure is 32 percent, and for high-poverty middle schools it is 44 percent.[24] These precise figures are recent, but the teacher qualification problem has been known for some time. We can only assume that the framers of the legislation knew in advance that states could not meet the requirements. They just didn't care.

Even classroom paraprofessionals must have completed two years of college and have an associate's degree or have passed a state test on content and teaching skills. New hires had to meet this requirement as of January 8, 2003; existing paraprofessionals have four years to ratchet up their credentials.

Paraprofessionals are low-salaried staff who often come from lower income neighborhoods. Many urban education experts contend that they are the best possible candidates to become accredited teachers—they are familiar with the situation and know what they're getting into and have shown that they can deal with it. But there is no federal money to assist them to their degrees, and if they should attain one, they will no doubt find more attractive salaries outside of the school, and better working conditions—NCLB greatly restricts what services they can provide to children. They can't teach, for instance, unless "directly supervised" by a teacher.

Harry Reid, the Democratic whip in the Senate is said to have gathered some education lobbyists together and asked, "How on earth could you have let this happen?" ("On earth" was not actually the phrase he used.) How, indeed? Well, money can be attractive and addictive. How else to explain Democrats George Miller and Ted Kennedy's willingness to endorse President Bush's proposal? Kennedy and Miller now complain that Bush didn't deliver the promised dollars—their versions contained $10 billion more than the $1.4 billion of new money actually appropriated.[25] Some states are already thinking that their costs—in dollars, not even counting hassle—might well be more than they get from NCLB. As noted earlier, William Mathis has projected that the cost to the states will run at least $84 billion and might run as much as $148 billion.

Thomas Gaffey, a state legislator in Connecticut says, "I'm sitting here shaking my head. I knew this was loaded with problems, but what the heck was going through their minds?"[26] What indeed? States should look at the lucre-drug that Bush and the NCLB are offering them and just say, "No!"

Notes

1. "Christopher Lee, "35 Senators Oppose Outsourcing Plan." *Washington Post,* February 5, 2003, p. A21.

2. Robert Tomsho, GOP's Election Gains Give Vouchers a Second Wind." *Wall Street Journal,* November 11, 2002, p. 1.

3. Valerie Strauss, "President to Push Vouchers for D. C." *Washington Post,* February 8, 2003, p. B2.

4. Sally West Johnson, "Mathis Rips Feds Over School Act." *Rutland Herald* (Vermont), February 5, 2003. The analysis can be obtained by e-mailing William Mathis at wmathis@sover.net.

5. William J. Mathis, "No Child Left Behind: What Are the Costs? Will We Realize Any Benefits?" *Phi Delta Kappan*, May 2003, pp. 679–86.

6. Robert L. Linn, "Standards-Based Accountability: Ten Suggestions." Policy Paper, Center for Research in Evaluation, Standards and Student Testing, 1998.

7. General Accounting Office, *Educational Achievement Standards: NAGB's Approach Yields Misleading Interpretations*. Washington, DC: Author, June 1993, Report GAO/PEMD-93-12.

8. National Academy of Sciences, *Grading the Nation's Report Card: Evaluating NAEP and Transforming the Assessment of Educational Progress*. Washington, DC: National Academy Press, 1999.

9. Lyle V. Jones, "National Tests of Educational Reform: Are They Compatible?" Princeton, NJ: Policy Information Center, Educational Testing Service, 1997. Accessible at www.ets.org/search97cgi/s97_cgi.

10. U.S. Department of Education, *The Nation's Report Card: Fourth Grade Reading 2000*. Washington, DC: Author, Report No. NCES 2001-499, p. 15.

11. Warwick P. Elley, *How in the World Do Students Read?* The Hague, Holland: International Association for the Evaluation of Educational Achievement, 1992. Available in the United States through the International Reading Association, Newark, Delaware.

12. Robert L. Linn, Eva L. Baker, and Damian W. Betebenner, "Accountability systems: Implications of the No Child Left Behind Act of 2001." *Educational Researcher*, August/September 2002, pp. 3–16.

13. Information can be found at the organization's websites, www.ncsl.org, and www.ccsso.org.

14. Randy Ross, "School Choice Where None Exists." *Education Week*, December 4, 2002, p. 37.

15. Thomas J. Kane and Douglas O Staiger, "Volatility in School Test Scores: Implications for Test-Based Accountability Systems." In Diane Ravitch (Ed.), *Brookings Papers on Education 2002*. Washington, DC: Brookings Institution, 2002.

16. Lynn Olson, "Study Questions Reliability of Single Year Test-Score Gains." *Education Week*, May 23, 2001 p. 9.

17. Karl L. Alexander, Doris R. Entwistle, and Linda S. Olson, "Schools, Achievement and Inequality: A Seasonal Perspective."

Educational Evaluation and Policy Analysis, Summer, 2001, pp. 171–91.

18. Tim Simmons, "U.S. Standards Perplex N.C. Schools." *Raleigh News & Observer,* June 2, 2002, p. A1.

19. Denis P. Doyle, "AYP Revealed, Now What?" *The Doyle Report,* June 4, 2002. "AYP Once More Once," *The Doyle Report,* June 13, 2002. Available at www.thedoylereport.com

20. Chester E. Finn, Jr., "Why America Has the World's Dimmest Bright Kids." *Wall Street Journal,* February 25, 1998, p. A22.

21. "The Editors: Slick Lamar." *The New Republic,* March 4, 1996.

22. Catherine Gewertz, "City Districts Seek Teachers with Licenses." *Education Week,* September 11, 2002, p. 1.

23. Kate Walsh, *Teacher Certification Reconsidered: Stumbling for Quality.* Baltimore, MD: The Abell Foundation, 2001.

24. *Education Week. Quality Counts 2003: If I Can't Learn from You . . . Ensuring a Highly Qualified Teacher in Every Classroom.* Bethesda, MD: Author, January 9, 2003.

25. Erik W. Robelen, "Democratic, GOP Education Plans Differ by Billions." *Education Week,* March 27, 2003, p. 1.

26. Robert A. Frahm, "Lawmakers Hear Criticism of Education Reform Law." *Hartford Courant,* February 8, 2003, p. 1.

A Surefire Way to Destroy America
Test Every Kid Every Year

You never know when a traumatic experience will come back to haunt you or, less often, when it might come back to provide some insight. A dire experience from over thirty-five years ago is just now yielding insights into the nature of American public education and how to destroy it. In 1965, while a graduate student, I spent a year in Hong Kong where I occasionally guest-lectured advanced undergraduates in psychology at Hong Kong University. On my first outing, I, being a product of my American culture, emulated my American teachers. I prepared a set of notes from which to lecture, but also some questions to stimulate thought and discussion.

When I asked my first question, the students sat there. I was a graduate student in psychology, not education, and so had not heard the phrase "wait time." But I had had some clinical psychology courses and knew that when the client was silent, it was unwise for the therapist to jump in. So, I stood and waited. They sat. I stood. They sat. They won. I went on with the talk. Another query also elicited only silence. The chairman of the psychology department was in the room for my talk, and when the class ended I asked, "What on earth happened?" He chuckled and said, "Oh, they were probably embarrassed that you didn't know the answers to the questions." In Hong Kong, professors profess; students absorb.

Recently, I recounted this tale to a professor in Taiwan, wondering if my long-ago experience still held. "Yes," he said. "Professors' questions are often met with stony silence." The insight is this: American kids ask questions. That has big payoffs for them and the country down the road. More about this later.

The recently completed TIMSS-R videotape study recorded teachers teaching in seven countries.[1] In Japan and Hong Kong, virtually all class time is filled with teacher talk. In the United States, and to a lesser extent, in other nations, the students often talk, ask questions, and interact with teachers. The silence of the students is hardly a trivial matter. In an article about why Japanese scientists rarely win Nobel Prizes, one Japanese scientist said, "Teachers still teach you that eloquence may be silver but silence is golden."[2]

In his book, *The Enigma of Japanese Power,* Dutch journalist and long-time Japan resident Karel van Wolferen told of a Japanese scientist who did win a Nobel Prize. Van Wolferen said that opinion in Japan was universal: The scientist, Susumu Tonegawa, would never have won had he stayed in Japan. The press for conformity to group norms would have prevented the individualist, high-risk researches that often lead down dead ends, but also, on occasion, result in a Nobel Prize. At the autobiography section of the Nobel website (http://www.nobel.se), Tonegawa states that his mentor at the University of Kyoto, where he took a bachelor's degree, gave him the best advice he ever got. It was, essentially, "Go East Young Man." Tonegawa went East to the United States, took his doctorate at the University of California, San Diego, and did his prize-winning research at MIT.

Nor is this just an East-and-West-never-meet story. In "At Least Our Kids Ask Questions," writer Amy Biancolli told a similar tale about her experiences teaching Shakespeare in Scotland.[3] Biancolli lamented, "It took months of badgering before I was able to get my Scottish teenagers to speak up in class. They simply weren't accustomed to asking questions or tossing around their own observations." Biancolli contrasts the silence of the Scots to

> "It took months of badgering before I was able to get my Scottish teenagers to speak up in class."

American classrooms: "American schools teach American kids to ask questions. They teach students to be curious, skeptical, even contrary, to ask for the whys and hows behind the whats in the rote acquisition of facts." Indeed. My daughter had teachers in *elementary school* who instructed her that there is no such thing as a bad question. She peppered me with them. I didn't think too much about it at the time, but I do now. Consider what twelve years in an environment that values and encourages questions does for a person's inquisitiveness in contrast to a dozen years spent in an environment that cherishes silence.

The opposite of asking questions is taking standardized tests. These tests force you to converge on a single, preselected, right answer while trying to fool you into picking a wrong one. These tests totally prevent curiosity or creativity or thoughtfulness. If you think while taking a test, you're in trouble. Thinking slows you down and you won't get to all of the questions. In fact, in its books that contain old SATs, the College Board also provides a set of test-taking guidelines. One says simply, "Keep moving."

> The opposite of asking questions is taking standardized tests.

In the 1980s, some American education reformers argued that we should adopt the Japanese model of education. Japan had high test scores and a booming economy. We had middling test scores and a slumping economy. People (wrongly) saw a causal connection: High test scores *produce* economic good times. We don't hear much about this anymore. Japanese kids (along with those in Singapore, South Korea, Hong Kong, and Taiwan) still score among the top nations on tests of math and science, but their country has suffered over a decade of recession.

For all their elevated test scores, the Asian nations do not receive superior rankings on global competitiveness from the high-powered think tank, the World Economic Forum (WEF) in Geneva. The United States is first out of the eighty ranked countries (Finland is ranked number two). Singapore, which usually has the highest test scores in the world is in fourth place. Taiwan is seventh, Japan 21st, Korea 23rd. To see if there were some

> For all their elevated test scores, the Asian nations do not receive superior rankings on global competitiveness from the WEF.

general relationship between test scores and competitiveness, I correlated the ranks of thirty-five nations whose children took tests in the Third International Mathematics and Science Study with their competitiveness ranks from the WEF. If test scores are important to competitiveness, as was asserted in 1983's "A Nation At Risk," the correlation should be high. It was +0.19—that is, virtually zero.

The WEF has a lot of subcategories within its overall competitiveness ranking, and one in which the United States remains number one is in the cluster of variables that the WEF calls "National Innovative Capacity." Standardized tests don't deal with innovation. Innovation comes from asking questions, being curious, and critically thinking about something—all those things at which Biancolli says American schools excel.

The No Child Left Behind Act of 2001 requires that all students be tested with standardized tests in reading and math, every year in grades three through eight. In two years science will be added. Schools must make adequate yearly progress (AYP), such that by 2001 all students reach the "proficient" level. In the great tradition of "The beatings will continue until morale improves," schools that fail to show AYP are subject to severe punishment. This ensures that a great deal of time will be spent preparing for the test and that a great deal of attention will be given to the results. Teachers will stifle thought, discussion, and question asking in the name and hope of raising test scores. Call it educational terrorism. I can't think of a better way to destroy the nation.

Notes

1. Patrick Gonzales, "Overview of the TIMMS-R Video Study." Presented at the annual convention of the American Educational Research Association, Chicago, IL, April 24, 2003.

2. Howard W. French, "Hypothesis: A Scientific Gap. Conclusion: Japanese Custom." *New York Times*, August 7, 2001. Over the last decade, Americans have won fifty Nobels, and Japanese residing in Japan, two. When one won in 2000, he was immediately appointed to head up a commission to increase the number of Japanese scientists who win Nobels.

3. *Washington Post*, April 27, 2001.

The Governors' Debacle
The High-Stakes Testing Movement

led by America's governors, the educational standards movement and its principal bludgeon, high-stakes testing, have produced an educational debacle. They did it all without the help
of that "weapon of mass destruction," the No Child Left Behind
Act of 2001. Assisted by the likes of William Bennett, Chester E.
Finn, Jr., Diane Ravitch, and their ilk, the governors have decided
to "gas" the kids. Finn, for example, in 2000 produced a report
that called many states "irresponsible" for their standards and
designated their standards as "lousy." He called them lousy in
spite of the fact that the states so labeled had the highest scores in
the country on the National Assessment of Educational Progress
and had outscored virtually all of the forty-one nations in the
Third International Mathematics and Science Study.

Consider these items from the boot camps formerly known as
schools:

- From the *Arizona Daily Star*, April 2, 2000: "She turned 10
last week. Her bed at home lies empty this morning as she
wakes in an unfamiliar bed at a psychiatric hospital. Anxiety
disorder. She had a nervous breakdown the other day. In
fourth grade." She told her parents she couldn't handle all

the pressure to do well on the tests. She was right to worry: On the previous administration, 90 percent of Arizona's kids flunked.

■ From the *San Francisco Examiner*, March 19, 2000: "When an East Palo Alto parent asked school district superintendent Charlie Mae Knight why there are no whale watching field trips this year, Knight replied, 'Kids are not tested on whale watching, so they're not going whale watching.'"

> *"Kids are not tested on whale watching, so they're not going whale watching."—Charlie Mae Knight*

■ From the *Norfolk (VA) Virginian Pilot,* March 21, 2000: "School Board members will discuss today whether they should institute mandatory recess for all elementary schools, in response to a campaign by parents to give their children a break between classes." Preparing for Virginia tests had so consumed most Virginia Beach schools, they had abandoned this traditional respite. The notion that children should have fun in school is now a heresy.

No recess and, in many cases, no art, no music, no social studies, no physical education. Nor are kids doing much of anything creative or interesting. From the Portland *Oregonian,* April 5, 1999: "Drill and practice. Multiple-choice questions. Teaching to the test. Dirty words. Or frowned-upon practices, at least, in the annals of teaching methods. And yet, with their principal's blessing, teachers at Portland's Binnsmead Middle School recently traded their usual creative styles of teaching for boring dittoed questions, multiple-choice answer grids and practice versions of standardized tests." One teacher, not yet under the high-stakes gun, is already making plans for what he will drop from his social studies classes: "mock trials, debates, projects, project presentations, constructive controversies, experiments, research, class discussions run by students, mock congress. In other words, all the fun stuff!"

> *One teacher is already making plans for what he will drop from his social studies classes: all the fun stuff!*

If these tests were well-constructed instruments that measured important material, we might tolerate these dire consequences, but all too often the tests are multiple-choice muddles testing trivia. At least, in those few instances in which we have seen them—the states have treated them as if they were intelligence reports on Al Qaeda and fired teachers who have dared reveal a few to interested parents. A Chicago teacher, reacting in horror to the low-quality Chicago exams, published four of them in a newspaper.

These tests contained mostly Trivial Pursuit–type items and worse: Many of them had no right answers, many had multiple right answers (although the instructions insisted there was only one such), they were full of cultural stereotypes, and some even contained factually erroneous history. Chicago Public Schools suspended the teacher without pay (by union rules, it could not fire him outright without a hearing) and sued him for $1.4 million, the ludicrous sum the district claims it will take to replace the 120 questions that appeared in the paper (if states and districts really pay $12,000 an item for tests, I think I've found a new profession).[1]

Maybe the kids in Chicago were lucky to be asked only trivia. In Virginia, tenth graders must "analyze the regional development of Asia, Africa, the Middle East, Latin America, and the Caribbean in terms of physical, economic, and cultural characteristics and historical evolution from 1000 A.D. to the present."[2] No doubt the reader's first response to this standard is, "Ohmigod, they left out Australia and New Zealand."

Despite asking students to demonstrate individually what university faculties cannot collectively, Virginia is an underachieving state. In South Dakota,

> Students will analyze the geographic, political, economic and social structures of the early civilization of ancient Greece with emphasis on the location and physical setting that supported the rise of this civilization; the connections between geography and the development of city-states, including patterns of trade and commerce; the transition from tyranny to oligarchy to early democratic patterns of government and the significance of citizenship; the differences between Athenian, or direct, democracy and representative democracy; the significance of Greek mythology in the everyday life of people in ancient Greece and its influence on modern literature and language; the similarities and differences between the life in Athens and Sparta; the rise of Alexander the Great in the north and the spread of Greek

culture; and the cultural contributions in the areas of art, science, language, architecture, government and philosophy.[3]

This is a sixth grade standard. Sixth grade. A time when boys are more concerned with the autocracy of testosterone than the democracy of Athens, and girls more interested in the topography of their bodies than the geography of Greece.

Needless to say, along with pressures to pass the tests come hours of homework. "It breaks a mother's heart to see her child in tears because they have so much homework that supper was the only break in the evening," said one Lincoln, Nebraska, mom in a *Newsday* article (April 2, 2000). "You can forget about ever doing anything as a family during the week," said another.

In only a few places do people receive praise for doing well on these tests. Mostly, people get punished for doing poorly. Kids get retained in grade and forced into after-school programs, Saturday programs, and summer school. Kids don't graduate. Teachers and principals get fired or transferred ("Test Scores May Write Principals' Pink Slips," heralded the *New York Post*, May 27, 1999). Schools lose their accreditation. The state takes over whole districts (as if the state had the expertise the districts lack!). Of course, the schools in jeopardy sit in poor neighborhoods. Using the previous year's test scores, the February 29, 2000, *Denver Post* looked to see which schools would have received an F if Governor Bill Owens' plan to award letter grades to schools had been in place. All but two had poverty rates of 75 percent or higher.

> *In only a few places do people receive praise for doing well on these tests.*

These circumstances produce a wide range of totally predictable outcomes. So far, there are only two documented low-score suicides (a ten-year-old in New York and an eleven-year-old in California), but many tales of third graders getting sick on test day. The Stanford 9 now comes with instructions on what to do if the child throws up on the answer sheet. "Two teachers allegedly helped students on the FCAT," headlined the *St. Petersburg Times* on March 9, 2000. The FCAT (Florida Comprehensive Achievement Test) is Florida's test championed by Governor Jeb Bush.

Well, some teachers might change scores to keep their jobs or to help kids they know don't take tests well, but others are voting with their feet. "We try to keep good teachers, but they're leaving in droves," said one person in Newport News, Virginia. It apparently has never occurred to those pushing the tests that taking the fun out of teaching exacerbates an already existing teacher shortage. We can only imagine how few students suffering through this regimen and watching their teachers suffer through it will react. Who on earth, looking at this situation, would want become a teacher? Indeed, one could view the whole scheme as one strategy in a plan to kill public education—make school such a miserable experience that the students, once grown up and raising their own families, will not want to surrender their own kids to the oppression.

There is more. "Pressure to boost scores leads schools to exclude weaker kids," noted *USA Today* on September 7, 1999. Want higher scores? Just designate more kids "special education" students and exclude them from the tests. (This is an additive to the old technique of encouraging certain children to stay home on test day.) Another new tack available to high school administrators—pack the kids off to a GED program. Then their test scores don't count against the school average.

"Indicted school official put on leave with pay," headlined the *Austin American-Statesman* on April 8, 1999. The official allegedly altered scores. Noting that this act qualified as a misdemeanor, some Texas legislators moved to make it a felony.

Texas' situation illustrates the sinister and purely political nature of high-stakes testing. In the March 28, 2000, issue of the *Baltimore Sun*, a story, "Validity of Texas Tests Questioned," revealed that a U.S. Department of Education study raising questions about the results was written under a pen name and has not yet been made available to the public.[4] Anything questioning then-governor George W. Bush's "Texas Miracle" was apparently too hot for federal hands to hold, although the *Sacramento Bee's* March 22, 2000, article, "More Muddle than Miracle," did just that. (Author's note: One wonders if Department of Education officials foresaw Bush moving from Austin to Washington and taking Houston Superintendent of Schools, Rod Paige, to head the department.)

Many more savage educational practices could be documented as a consequence of high-stakes testing, but these will suffice for the moment. Beginning in 1989, the governors, meeting with then-president George H. W. Bush at the first education "summit," started the machinations that have led to this debacle. Periodic other summits kept the momentum going. Pushed by Engler in Michigan, Thompson in Wisconsin, Voinovich in Ohio, Carlsson in Minnesota, Owens in Colorado, Allen in Virginia, Wilson and Davis in California, Weld and Celucci in Massachusetts, and the Bushes in Texas and Florida, the high-standards–high-stakes movement has become a medieval instrument of torture for tormenting a whole generation of kids. The ultimate victim of this catastrophe is childhood itself (see "The End of Childhood," Chapter 23).

The governors, now aware that many parents are incensed about what they have wrought, have become frightened about a loss of support, votes, and money. They are planning schemes to dodge their responsibility for the debacle and to dump it onto the already sagging shoulders of education administrators, as if it were their idea all along. The governors shouldn't be allowed to get away with that. (The governors enjoyed a reprieve in the form of George W. Bush's education legislation. Now they can claim that they are just following the law. The debacle has grown worse. See "The No Child Left Behind Act, a Plan for the Destruction of Public Education: Just Say No" Chapter 1.)

Notes

1. CPS later fired the teacher, a thirty-year veteran. In early 2003, the Chicago Board of Education, having spent four years and over $1,000,000 prosecuting the case and having cost the teacher $130,000 in legal fees, reduced the claim to $500. CPS will receive this minuscule sum only if all of the teacher's appeals on First Amendment grounds fail.

2. Standards in their original form may be found at: Virginia, www.pen.k12.va.us/VDOE/Superintendant/Sols.home/shtml.

3. www.state.sd.us/deca/ta/contentstandards/index.htm.

4. In the fall of 2003, it has still not been made public.

4 Failing Children—Twice

As president, Clinton called for an end to "social promotion." If the kids aren't cutting it, hold them back in the same grade. The *Washington Post*'s syndicated columnist E. J. Dionne worries that retaining children in grade might turn out to be just another gimmick. It is worse. It is a disaster. Given the increasing popularity of using failure as a pedagogical technique, it is important to know this about retaining children in grade: It doesn't work.

Unlike most aspects of education, which have contending forces pulling in opposite directions, the body of research on flunking kids speaks with a single voice.[1] One 1992 study reviewed the research literature on forty-nine educational innovations, calculated their impact on achievement, and then ranked them in order of power.[2] Retention in grade ranked 49th. It was among the few innovations that actually produced negative results. I recently reviewed and updated this research literature, adding studies not available to the 1992 analysis. Nothing has changed.

> *Retaining children in grade is a disaster.*

Why do people think failing kids works? In large part because most people are not in a position to conduct a controlled experiment. Teachers and parents usually can see only how retained children fare the next year. They do better—on the same material they did poorly on the first time around. A little better. Few blossom into high achievers. Teachers and parents, watching the children struggle in the second year in the same grade, then assume, reasonably, that the children's situation would have been that much worse had they been promoted.

But there have been situations in which some children who had low achievement were promoted, while other children of the same low achievement were flunked. In those settings, the children who were promoted fared at least as well, usually better, than those who were left behind.

Retention is often presented as the only alternative to "social promotion" or promotion for "seat time." In fact, it is nothing more than a way of pretending to do something for a child without actually doing anything—except make the kid pay with another year in school, surrounded by a group of strangers, mostly younger than the flunked child.

> Some have declared that they need the threat of retention to make children work hard in school.

Some have declared that they need the threat of retention to make children work hard in school. The administrators and teachers who make this claim seem not to realize that it is a stunning admission of incompetence, as if they have nothing else in their motivational arsenals.

And, of course, these teachers and administrators—not to mention politicians like President Clinton—are left with nothing to say when presented with the school systems of Japan and much of Europe that do not retain—or track—children at all before the differentiated curricula of high school. In international comparisons, these systems score as well or better than the United States on everything except reading, where only Finland scores higher—their "social promotion" doesn't damage achievement. When I discussed retention with Danish educators while spending a summer in Denmark, they said they considered retention in grade a barbaric practice, something that would be practiced only by a primitive culture that didn't really like its children.

And it is true that retention has significant negative emotional outcomes in this country. One study found that kids rated their fear of retention in grade just behind that of losing a parent or going blind.[3] Other studies, while not so dramatic, typically find that retained children say they are "upset" or "sad" about it. No study has found that retention does wonders for self-esteem.

So, what to do for low-achieving students? From an analysis of the research data, the answer seems to be this: Provide these children with extra assistance—summer school if need be (something that is a lot less expensive than having the child repeat the same grade the next year)—and then promote. Retention in grade is a practice that has no place in any society that thinks of itself as humane, as doing its best by its children.

Whenever a district or state proposes tougher rules for retention, some folks express concern about the increased cost of retaining lots of children. They *should* worry. Retaining children in elementary school greatly increases the probability of their becoming truant in middle school and dropping out from high school. The good citizens will get their money back in the short term when the kids leave school before graduating, but pay many times over when these students end up on welfare or in prison.

> *Retaining children in elementary school greatly increases the probability of their becoming truant in middle school and dropping out from high school.*

In the four years since this article appeared in *Education Week*, retention in grade has become more prevalent as state or district policy. Sometimes it is a well-intentioned reform. At other times, it is simply a cynical ploy to raise test scores. If a state tests children in the fourth grade, it can raise scores by retaining children it thinks will score poorly in the third grade. There is no evidence that such a policy produces any long-term benefit.

Notes

1. This research was summarized by Lorrie Shepard and Mary Lee Smith, editors of *Flunking Grades: Research and Policies on Retention*. London: Falmer, 1989.

2. John A. Hattie, "Towards a Model of Schooling: A Synthesis of Meta-analyses." *Australian Journal of Education*, January, 1992, pp. 5–13.

3. See Shepard and Smith.

Kindergarten Is Too Late

Editors at the *Washington Post* once endorsed a proposal for full-day kindergarten in one of the area's suburbs. In the end, I would probably concur that it's a good idea, but I have two concerns. First, the proposal, as presented, was yet another attack in the war on childhood. *Kindergarten* is German for "children's garden," and initially it was indeed a place where children's developmental needs were taken care of and kids could grow and flower. People understood that young children don't think the same as we do, that they were not just small grown-ups.

Now, kindergarten become a more regimented mini first grade, complete with homework (!?!?) for the miniature adults who attend. I doubt seriously that anyone in kindergarten today would ever be tempted, in maturity, to write a book such as, *Everything I Needed to Know, I Learned in Kindergarten.* Today it would be more like *Everything I Needed to Know About Letter–Sound Correspondences and How to be Burned Out as a Learner by Third Grade, I Learned in Kindergarten.*

My other objection is almost the converse of the first: It is that for a substantial number of children, those living in poverty, it is already too late. For instance, pregnant women in poverty often do not receive prenatal care in the first trimester, with devastating outcomes for their children. The outcome easiest to observe is low birth weight. A large study (340,000 children) in Florida found that low birth weight was associated with all types of mental deficits but seemed to have its greatest impact on the most severe syndromes.[1] Black children, male children, and children of poor or single mothers were most at risk.

> *For a substantial number of children, those living in poverty, kindergarten is already too late.*

There are other deficits that show up where the cause is not so specific or readily determined. I once analyzed some test scores of children entering the first grade. For verbal and mathematics tests, the gaps between white students on the one hand and black and Hispanic students on the other were already huge. For tests involving the kinds of spatial-perceptual skills that can be acquired navigating the physical environment, the differences were much reduced, and black and Hispanic children scored much better. Because many of the black and Hispanic kids were also poor, the implication was that they did not live with well-educated parents who could provide them rich linguistic and numerical stimulation.

One study found that middle class parents spoke to their children at four times the rate that poor parents did.[2] And this study did not try to examine the complexity of the utterances. Another study, by Betty Hart and Todd Risley, found that mothers with professional-level education used many more words in interacting with their children than did poor mothers. In fact, the *children* of the professional mothers used more words than the mothers on welfare used when talking with their children.[3] The interactions of the mothers on welfare with their children were much more often negatively charged. This confirms my informal observations in a grocery store I used to frequent. A lot of poor parents used this store, and their communications with their children seemed to consist of two commands: "Come here!" and "Shut up!" If these orders did not produce the desired result, they were repeated at increasing volume, often terminating in harshly grabbed wrists or slapped fannies.

> *One study found that middle class parents spoke to their children at four times the rate that poor parents did.*

Back in the 1960s, English linguist, Basil Bernstein, described my experience more formally, referring to the "restricted code" of

words used by working-class parents in contrast to the "elaborated code" of middle-class parents. Because Bernstein was a
product of class-ridden England and because it was the 1960s and
because American educators were trying to erase class and ethnic
differences in intelligence and achievement, when Bernstein's
ideas crossed the Atlantic, they quickly died from political incor-
rectness. They should be reexamined, and there is some indication that they are coming to researchers' attention again.

Given low birth weights and the other accompaniments of
poverty, it is little wonder that the U.S. Department of Education's
study of kindergartners found that poverty profoundly affected
cognitive development in different groups.[4] The study did not
measure poverty directly, but used proxy variables such as
mother's educational level. On a test of reading, kindergartners
whose mothers did not have a high school diploma did not do
well: 43 percent of white kindergartners, 53 percent of blacks, 28
percent of Asians, and 64 percent of Hispanics finished in the bottom 25 percent of all tested. Similar results turned up for mathematics and general knowledge.

Overall, 18 percent of white kindergartners scored in the lowest 25 percent of all scorers, while 30 percent scored in the highest quartile. For blacks, 34 percent were in the bottom quartile, 15
percent in the highest. A 1998 book, *The Black-White Test Score
Gap,*[5] dealt with differences at the elementary and secondary levels, but the differences are there before the kids ever start school.
The good news is that the same study that implicated low birth
weight in mental deficiency also found that it was the kids'
impoverished environment that hindered mental development
the most. That's good news, because, theoretically, we have the
means to alter those environments.

Around 1990, analyses by some education reformers proposed just such alterations, with the school serving as the focal
point for change. The idea was to turn schools into comprehensive childcare systems. Because the schools are established institutions in the neighborhood and are accessible, why send parents,
who often lack easy access to transportation or the money to pay
for it, all over town to obtain various social services? Why
indeed? The school could become a one-stop shop for them.

I'm not sure why these proposals were never realized, but a
couple of conjectures seem plausible: I think they were the vic-

tims of the twin debacles of Outcomes-Based Education and the Clinton Health Care proposal. No matter what the merits of these two programs might have been, they came to represent horrible examples of Big Government sticking its nose into places where it had no business. The idea of cradle-to-diploma comprehensive childcare came to look like government regimentation.

Of course, without a return to the view of the child as a creature to be nurtured rather than as "raw material" to be molded into a "product" that will happily and obediently make widgets and profits for some corporation all of his or her adult life, extending the domain of the school would only make things worse. Still, these comprehensive proposals need to be revisited. Perhaps we could even convince business and industry that it is in their enlightened self-interest to invest in the care of children from conception on. Perhaps if we invested in prenatal and infant care and teaching impoverished parents about what a growing brain needs, we could stop building so many prisons. See also Chapter 25, "Long-Term Studies of Preschool: The Benefits Far Outweigh the Costs."

> *Perhaps if we invested in prenatal and infant care and teaching impoverished parents about what a growing brain needs, we could stop building so many prisons.*

Notes

1. Michael Resnick et al. "Risk Factors from Low Birth Weights." *Pediatrics,* December, 1999.

2. Cited in Richard Rothstein, *The Way We Were?* New York, Century Foundation Press, 1998.

3. Betty Hart and Todd R. Risley, *Meaningful Differences in the Everyday Experience of Young American Children.* Baltimore, MD: Paul H. Brookes, 1995.

4. National Center for Education Statistics, *America's Kindergartners.* Washington, DC, 2000. Report No. NCES 2000-070. A more comprehensive analysis of the data appeared in Valerie E. Lee and David T. Burkam's *Inequality at the Starting Gate.* Washington, DC: Economic Policy Institute, 2002.

5. Christopher Jencks and Meredith Phillips, eds, *The Black–White Test Score Gap.* Washington, DC: Brookings Institution Press, 1998.

6   Testing Flunks Life

In Alexandria, Virginia, in 2001, the city was trying to decide what to do with some undeveloped and extremely valuable Potomac River property between two developments of million-dollar townhomes. One option was a school to teach disadvantage children—of which there are a lot in Alexandria—how to build boats. One townhouse resident told the *Washington Post* why she didn't want to build that school in her toney neighborhood: It's a feel-good activity, she said. If boat building raised test scores, schools would be building boats all across the nation. Problem is, she's probably right. Anything a school wants to try has to pass a test: Will it raise test scores? If not, forget it. Nothing else counts. Trips to see whales, canceled. Museum visits, canceled. Arts, physical education, social studies, all gone—victims of the need to raise test scores. *Whatever Happened to Recess?* asked the title of a Susan Ohanian book.

All of this is too much, yet President George W. Bush layered an enormous new helping of testing with the No Child Left Behind Act: every kid, every year, in grades 3 through 8 in reading and math, with science to be added in two years. It will cost the states much more to develop their tests than they will collect from Mr. Bush.

Given this testing juggernaut, perhaps we should stop bubbling in answer sheets for just a moment, collect our breath, and reflect on some things the tests that dominate our schools do not measure:

Creativity	Self-discipline
Critical thinking	Empathy
Resilience	Leadership
Motivation	Compassion
Persistence	Sense of beauty
Curiosity	Sense of wonder
Humor	Integrity
Reliability	Courage
Enthusiasm	Cowardice
Civic-mindedness	Resourcefulness
Self-awareness	

These are the things that matter in life, the things that count. Test scores don't predict success on the job. They certainly don't predict success in life. In fact, even the test *designed* to predict success in the freshman year of college, the College Board's SAT, doesn't do a particularly good job of it. The College Board's own data show that the SAT misses 80 percent of what determines freshman college grades—that is, 80 percent of what makes the difference between making the dean's list and flunking out is due to personal qualities the SAT doesn't measure.

> *Even the test designed to predict success in the freshman year of college, the College Board's SATs, doesn't do a particularly good job of it.*

College admissions officers know this. For them, the SAT is convenient because it's free. If you ask a convention of admissions officers, "How many of you would continue to use the SAT if your institution had to pay for it?" you won't see any hands in the air. Even admissions officers at selective universities such as Brown know it. Brown could fill over two freshman classes solely with kids who score between 750 and a perfect 800 on the SAT verbal. In 2001, it admitted only 29 percent of such students; it admitted 5 percent of those who scored lower than 450 and 7 percent of those who scored between 450 and 490. When the Bush administration decided to join with the plaintiffs in attacking the University of Michigan's affirmative action admissions plan, papers reported how Michigan does it. Of 150 total possible points, the ACT or SAT count for only twenty. Media made a big to do about Mount Holyoke's abandoning the SAT in its admissions process, but Holyoke officials pointed out it was no big deal: The test only counted for 10 percent of applicants' total admissions score.

As for jobs, Henry Levin of Columbia University studied the relationship between test scores and employment and concluded that "the link [between jobs and test scores] is so small that when test scores are used for employment selection there is a high probability that many workers will be rejected for jobs that they could perform and selected for jobs that they cannot perform."[1]

Fortunately, despite the urgings of the Business Round Table and the National Alliance of Manufacturers, employers still know tests' failings. Alan Wurtzel, chairman of the board at Circuit City, a large electronics discount retailer, captured the employer's perspective nicely in a *Washington Post* op-ed: "In hiring new employees for our stores, warehouses, and offices, Circuit City is looking for people who are able to provide very high levels of customer service, who are honest and who have a positive, enthusiastic, achievement-oriented work ethic."[2] That's it. Show up reliably and on time, be nice to the customers and other employees, don't do drugs, and get the customers to buy. Those abilities will get you a lot farther than some state's stamp on the back of your diploma certifying that you aced the state's tests.

> *Being able to deal with people will get you a lot farther than some state's stamp on the back of your diploma certifying that you aced the state's tests.*

Even testing people know that, in the long run, tests don't count. Thirty years ago, two researchers at the American College Testing Program looked for the link between success on tests and success later on.[3] They couldn't find one. And they lamented the way tests had affected our perceptions of academic skills and of ourselves:

One of the undesirable by-products of testing practice has been the emphasis on academic talent with its accompanying indifference to other kinds of talent. Tests have fostered a narrow conception of ability and restricted the diversity of talent which might be brought to the attention of young people considering various professions. It is small wonder that some people have mistakenly interpreted test scores as a measure of personal worth and have mistakenly assumed that academic talent, as evidenced in school, is related in a major way to later adult accomplishment.

Let's repeat that message: Test scores are not a measure of your worth, nor are they related to what you will accomplish as an adult. If President Bush had really wanted to help education, he would have given us reforms calling for less testing, not more.

> *Test scores are not a measure of your worth, nor are they related to what you will accomplish as an adult.*

Notes

1. Henry M. Levin, "High Stakes Testing and Economic Productivity," in Gary Orfield and Mindy L. Kornhaber, eds., *Raising Standards or Raising Barriers?* New York: The Century Foundation Press, 2001, pp. 39–50.

2. "Getting from School to Work," December 7, 1993, p. A25.

3. Leo Munday and Jean Davis, "Varieties of Accomplishment After College: Perspectives on the Meaning of Academic Talent." Research Report #62: American College Testing Program, Iowa City, IA, 1974.

7   The Malevolent Tyranny of Algebra

uick, when was the last time you solved a quadratic equation? Quick, given $ax^2 + bx + c = 0$, derive the formula for solving quadratic equations. What does *quadratic* mean, anyway? (Hint: It's not the same as in "quadraphonic.")

Quadratic equations are something that students learn when they take a subject called algebra. Although people have long said that there will be prayer in school as long as there is algebra, today, algebra rules. If physics is the Queen of Sciences, algebra is currently the King of All It Surveys.

Although algebra is all about finding values in equations, it has no value for most people. Its actual uselessness in most people's lives was wonderfully revealed in a *Washington Post* article from several years back. The story described how parents in Fairfax County, Virginia, were rushing home from work, bolting down dinner, and going to school to learn . . . algebra. "They came not for their benefit," the reporter wrote. "They had learned algebra years ago and most of them had no use for X's and Y's in their current lives."

That sure gives the game away: "Most of them had no use for X's and Y's in their current lives." Yet, they are inflicting those useless X's and Y's on themselves for the second time. This time, they're doing it so they can help their kids get through algebra. Apparently, it didn't occur to these parents to ask, "If I didn't need it, why am I suffering through it again just to help my kid successfully suffer through it?"

Why has algebra taken on such dimensions lately? Why do students in Virginia have to take algebra to graduate from high school? Why does the Montgomery County, Maryland, schools superintendent, Jerry Weast, fret over the failure rate on his algebra test? Why did Lee Stith, the president of the National Council of Teachers of Mathematics (NCTM), recently tell Brigid Shulte, a *Post* reporter, that "algebra is the civil rights issue of the new millennium, because it is that critical"?

> *Why has algebra taken on an aura of such importance lately? Because the entire nation has been algebra scammed.*

Why? Because virtually the whole nation has been algebra-scammed. Said Mr. Weast, "No algebra means no SAT test. No SAT test means limited college choice" (never mind that even the most selective colleges admit a wide range of SAT scores, and never mind that, in terms of later earnings, it doesn't matter what college you attended). Even the reporter fell for it and wrote, "Algebra is the gateway to college and higher-paying careers in a new technical world." Nonsense. Balderdash.

How did we come to think that algebra is important in kids' high school careers? Because of a foible of the human brain. Our brains appear to be hard-wired to make causal inferences from mere correlations. No doubt from an evolutionary perspective, this is generally a good thing, because it allows us to see patterns in our lives and in nature. But, as psychologists early demonstrated, we often see causes when they don't inhere. We infer causes where only correlations exist.

Psychologists demonstrated this many years ago. They showed a circle of light—call it A—moving across a screen and touching a second circle of light—call it B. If circle B then moved within a certain period of time, people watching the lights said that A caused B to move. If there were a delay of some seconds, then people said that B moved independently of A. We are especially wont to infer causality if event A is always followed by event B, and if B never occurs unless A does first. Actually, all this was worked out over two centuries ago by the British philosopher

David Hume, but he didn't have the technology to demonstrate it. He probably also didn't realize the long periods over which humans infer causality, as with sex and the appearance of infants or, for some on the Right, the '60s and the appearance of all current problems.

So it was that a few years ago, the College Board noticed that kids who take algebra (circle of light A), especially kids who take algebra in the eighth or ninth grade, also tended to take rigorous high school curricula and to go to college (circle of light B). "Aha!" said the board. They saw a correlation between algebra and later attainment. They then leapt to a causal conclusion: Algebra is a "gateway" course. Having observed the correlation between taking algebra and going on to college, the board inferred that there was a causal relationship. Nonsense. Balderdash.

What happens is this: Schools, whether we like it or not, are sorting machines. Jefferson proposed them as such, and they will function that way until some magical elixir can tune up the neurons in everyone's heads. Schools identify academic talent in kids. Children that teachers think are talented get algebra in the eighth grade, and those that have some talent, in the ninth grade. Those the school thinks have less ability tangle with quadratics in a later grade or not at all.

Is the school's ability to identify talent flawless? Of course not. Indeed, the reason that the NCTM's Mr. Stith casts algebra as a civil rights issue is that minority students are underrepresented in algebra classes in the eighth and ninth grades. And some kids, of any ethnicity, who are quiet and shy might get overlooked because they have not shown their teachers all they've got.

But is forcing everyone to take algebra the answer? Of course not. It is more likely to turn kids off math, and even off school altogether, than to identify hidden talent. If I were a school official in Virginia or Montgomery County, Maryland, I'd start looking for a correlation between forcing kids to take algebra and increased dropout rates.

Forcing everyone to take algebra is more likely to run more kids off math and even off school entirely than it is likely to identify hidden talent.

Already, we have some suggestive evidence from Milwaukee, which has had an algebra-for-all program for six years. Dennis Redovich, a retired educator who runs the Center for the Study of Jobs and Education in Wisconsin, tells me that 40 percent of Milwaukee ninth graders fail algebra, and that ninth graders constitute more than 40 percent of Milwaukee's dropouts. According to Mr. Redovich, the ninth grade in Milwaukee schools has been getting larger each year, largely as a result of students' failing algebra and lacking enough credits to become tenth graders. For instance, in 1998–1999, the ninth grade contained 9,340 students, but the tenth grade only 6,048 and the twelfth grade only 3,874.

Says Mr. Redovich, "Only 60 percent of the students who take algebra pass it. The kids fail algebra, sit around in 9th grade until they're 16 or 17 and then just disappear. Some will hang on until they reach the legal age for dropping out, 18." Some of the data seem to corroborate his contentions: If one subtracts the number of total dropouts from the ninth grade enrollment, almost 30 percent of the ninth graders are simply unaccounted for by the twelfth grade. I hear the sound of opening doors but it comes not from doors to opportunity, but to the school exits.

The dumbest slogan to come down the educational pike in recent years is "All children can learn." This meaningless cliché has not been elevated to mean, in the case of algebra, that all students can learn to the same high standard. This will happen about the same time that all students run a four-minute mile.

We can do better, no doubt. The place to start is elementary school, not the eight or ninth grade. There are also many other reasons for taking algebra that have nothing to do with jobs or college. Taught well (which it often isn't), algebra can reveal a language of relationships and the beauty and elegance of mathematics. It can actually be an aesthetic experience.

Moreover, learning everything you can about everything you can is a good strategy in school, because life after school contains so many uncertainties. You can't possibly know what you might need one day. I've needed some algebra in my field but haven't used calculus once in the forty-two years since the final exam. (Jobwise, only 4 percent of the population actually needs advanced mathematics.) Had I entered a more quantitative branch of psychology, though, calculus would have been inte-

Thinking that cramming algebra into all kids' heads is the means to a better life for them is drawing a bad causal inference from a mere correlation.

gral. French, taken only because that's what kids in the college track did when I was in school, turned out to be essential when I lived in France and extremely useful when I moved to Spain and then to Italy and learning those languages, because Spanish and Italian closely resemble French. And so forth. But thinking that cramming algebra into all kids' heads is the means to a better life for them is drawing a bad causal inference from a mere correlation.

8

Schools Should *Not* Prepare Students for the World of Work

Abstract

The work of schools is not the world of work. Schools should prepare children to live rich, generous lives in the hours they are freed from work.

Reading these words some seven years after they were written is depressing. Things have only gotten worse. The corporatization (and militarization) of schools continues. The conception of education expressed by Israel Sheffler (described in the article) seems more remote than ever.

When I give speeches around the country, by far the most common buzz-phrase I hear these days is "school-to-work transition," a distressing indicator of the increasing corporate control of education (government long ago surrendered). I believe that paying attention to this transition is a disaster in the making for schools.

Listen for a moment to what one employer, Alan Wurtzel, Chairman of the Board of Circuit City, an electronics discount firm, says he is looking for: "In hiring new employees for our stores and warehouses, Circuit City is looking for people who are able to provide very high levels of customer service, who are honest, and who have a positive, enthusiastic, achievement-oriented work ethic." What Wurtzel failed to say was that to people possessing all these qualities, Circuit City offers its warehouse staff $4.25 an hour (the minimum wage at the time) while members of the sales staff work strictly on commission.

Wurtzel's attitude is widespread: Employers demand a great deal for what they hand out. Their attitude was well captured in a "Frank and Ernest" cartoon, in which a company personnel officer tells Frank and Ernest, "What we're looking for is someone smart enough to pass our aptitude test and dumb enough to work for the pay we offer." Another cartoon, this one in the May 2003 issue of the cartoon monthly, *Funny Times,* shows a man looking at the reader. He says, "My dad used to tell me that I could pick a profession that was *fun,* or one that was *well-paid.* But I fooled *him!* I found one that was *neither!"*

The old saying, "The business of America is business," has lately been rendered as "The business of schools is business." What has been lost in all the rhetoric is that schools have no business with business. They should not be preparing students for the world of work. That schools are preparing students for the world of work represents a massive triumph of propaganda that would thrill both Pavlov and B. F. Skinner. For three administrations, millions of young people have been kept out of the labor force in the name of keeping inflation low. That they are cynical should not surprise us. That they have not risen up in revolt should.

The Concept of Work

We used to make fun of the Russians and their "glorious worker" propaganda. But we glorify the concept of work in this country just as propagandistically—just more subtly and more successfully (what we really glorify, of course, is capital). In fact, as John Kenneth Galbraith points out in *The Culture of Contentment*, we hide all jobs under the single glorious rubric of "work," ignoring the fact that much of "work" is ugly, hard, demeaning, and dangerous.

> We hide all our jobs under the single glorious rubric of "work," ignoring the fact that much of "work" is ugly, hard, demeaning, and dangerous.

Surveys have repeatedly found that most jobs are dull and boring, with no intrinsic meaning. Should schools collude in the preparation of students to endure the boredom of meaningless, small, repetitive, dull, unhealthy tasks? I don't think so. Work is as nasty as it is unavoidable, and we should realize that and treat it as such, not pretend it is something wonderful.

Evidence for this contention can be seen in the stunning popularity of the cartoon strip "Dilbert." The strip is currently seen in eight hundred newspapers. "Dilbert" is set in one of the most awful work settings imaginable. In one strip, Dilbert proposes to a co-worker that they quit and set up their own business. "Why quit?" asks the co-worker. "We can run our new company from our cubicles and get paid, too." Dilbert asks, "Wouldn't that be immoral?" The co-worker answers, "That's only an issue for people who aren't already in hell." Since putting his Internet address on line three years ago, "Dilbert" author Scott Adams has been besieged with letters offering insights but often asking, "How did you find out where I worked?" Apparently a lot of other people also think they're already in hell.

The alliance between business and schools is itself an alliance made in hell. It calls for schools to perform a massive job of conditioning students to be docile. (Getting fifty million kids to show up at the same place—school—on time everyday is itself a mammoth achievement of docility training.) To then claim that schools ought to be teaching students to be critical thinkers is ludicrous and hypocritical. The last thing an employer wants is someone who thinks critically. Critical thinkers will challenge the idiotic rules laid down by businesses. See "Dilbert" for wonderful examples of idiotic rules and challenges.

The Supply Side

In fact, schools have done a marvelous job on the supply side of the work force, but business and industry have done an absolutely lousy job on the demand side. And all the while, as a 1994 article in the *New York Times* reported, the productivity of the American worker, already the highest in the world, is rising.[1] Yet, in September 1993, Richard Barnet penned an article entitled simply "The End of Jobs." Although the United

> *Schools have done a marvelous job on the supply side of the work force, but business and industry have done an absolutely lousy job on the demand side.*

States, according to the *Times*, is the low-cost producer of many goods and services, jobs are disappearing. At least, good jobs are. In 1992, manufacturing, where the good jobs are, lost 255,000 jobs.[2] The restaurant industry alone added 249,000. Not many were for executive chefs. People went wild on March 8, 1992 when the Department of Labor announced that 705,000 jobs had been created in February, more new jobs than in any month in more than a decade. Little noticed was the comment that accompanies all these announcements: "Most of the new jobs were in the service sector."[3]

A Jeff McNelly cartoon in the *Chicago Tribune* captured the situation well. He depicted an after-dinner speaker saying, "The current economic recovery has produced 7.8 million jobs." At the same time, the busboy clearing the table thinks to himself, "And I have three of them." The busboy is lucky. After a reading of Jeremy Rifkin's *The End of Work*, I thought of a line from Kurt Vonnegut's 1965 novel on the deadly effects of automation: "The problem is, how to love people who have no use."

In the "Second Bracey Report on the Condition of Education," I noted that 26 percent of our college graduates take jobs that require no college. A few weeks later, another article put the figure at 31 percent. Barnet comments, "I have visited a variety of highly automated factories in Europe and the United States including automobile, electronics, and printing plants. The scarcity of human beings in these places is spooky." Productivity is rising, wages are falling. Not good.

Said NPR reporter David Maupus on "All Things Considered," "In today's economy, we should all think of ourselves as temps." Indeed, one need not be a Marxist economist to view the call for the schools to raise students to ever higher levels of skill as a strategy to drive down the wages of skilled labor.

The Work of Schools

If the work of schools is not the world of work, what then? How about a renewed emphasis on the school's civic function? Thomas Jefferson saw education as the means of protecting us from our government: "In every government on earth is some trace of human weakness, some germ of corruption and degeneracy which cunning will discover, and wickedness insensibly open, cultivate, and improve. Every government degenerates when trusted to the rulers over the people alone. The people themselves therefore are its only safe depositories. And rend even them safe, their minds must be improved somewhat."

For most of our history, schools concerned themselves primarily with this civic function. Surely Jefferson would be appalled at the corporate control of government, at our government-by-special interest, and at our low voter turnout. He would probably see them as failures of our educational system.

> *Jefferson would have been appalled at the corporate control of government, at our government-by-special interest, and at our low voter turnout.*

Vocational concerns crept into schools only when the move began toward universal secondary education. As this movement really got underway, it coincided with the development of testing by such theoreticians and zealots and racists as Lewis Terman, H. H. Goddard, Arthur Otis, Robert Yerkes, Carl Campbell Brigham, and E. L. Thorndike. Looking at their bell curves, these psychometricians concluded that it would be inhumane to present the same curriculum to all students. Low ability students *deserved* an easier course of study.

We are now in an era in which another buzz-phrase is "All children can learn to high standards" and ability grouping is out (in theory). What kind of education ought we to offer all children? Philosopher of education, Israel Sheffler, defines education as "the formation of habits of judgment and the development of character, the elevation of standards, the facilitation of understanding, the development of taste and discrimination, the stimulation of curiosity and wondering, the fostering of style and a sense of beauty, the growth of a thirst for new ideas and visions of the yet unknown."

That sounds good to me—a liberal education, one that liberates. Schools should prepare children to live rich, generous lives in the hours that they are freed from work. They can be trained for jobs after they finish their education. This must be possible: As noted, study after study finds U.S. workers the most productive in the world. It is when U.S. workers leave their job sites and become Joe and Josie Sixpacks that trouble begins. An education that would put most television out of business for lack of viewers would be a good start toward a good Sheffler-type education.

And what of vocational concerns? If high school grads drift into college without knowing why, wouldn't it be even more dangerous to let them drift into the job market where access to information is so much more difficult to come by? Well, yes. But why try to solve this problem during the high school years? Why not specialized centers that receive students after they complete high school? Would it not be possible for vocational educators to provide much richer and more valuable information to students when they're not competing with the rest of the high school for their attention? When they can have the kids all day long?

Certainly these young people are not needed by the market. People who can steer students toward what good jobs there are are valuable people. But is not some of their value squandered or at least diluted by operating through the high schools? Seems reasonable to me. I'd be interested in knowing what the people in the trenches think.

Notes

1. Sylvia Nasar, "The American Economy, Back on Top," *New York Times*, February 27, 2003, p. 1.

2. Jobs continued to increase during the Clinton years. During the Bush administration, well over two million jobs have been lost, as of Spring, 2003. As commencement 2003 approached, newspapers, magazines, and electronic media all featured articles on how tough it was going to be for the new grads to find decent jobs.

3. During the first eighteen months of George W. Bush's administration, 2.5 million jobs disappeared.

9   Poverty Issues Get Short Shrift

This essay first appeared in *USA Today* on November 2, 1999. It remains current. In 2002, the Bush administration appropriated $1.4 billion dollars in new federal aid to education as part of the No Child Left Behind Act. Most of this money is supposed to go to low-income schools, but it is a paltry sum spread across fifty states. Worse, it might cost the states as much as $148 billion to carry out the act—this at a time when everyone admits that state budgets are in their worst shape since World War II. For example, the projected deficits are $2 billion in Maryland, $10 billion in Texas, and $36 billion in California. Only Wyoming has a surplus. The $1.4 billion does not come with generous sentiments. As pundit George F. Will noted, the act is not really a carrot, but a stick. Its principal activity is to shame schools into high performance by calling them failures.[1] Know what? I don't think it will work (see Chapter 1, "The No Child Left Behind Act, a Plan for the Destruction of Public Education: Just Say No").

As a presidential candidate in 1999, Bill Bradley put forth a plan to deal with child poverty, a condition much more prevalent in the United States than in any other industrialized nation. He was the only candidate then or since to try to cope with the problem directly. At the 1999 "Education Summit," for instance, the assembled governors and business stood stonily silent on it.

Faced with the chronically low performance of poverty-ridden schools, some people—even some educators—say, "Poverty is not an excuse" and point to a few exceptional kids and a few exceptional schools as proof (see Chapter 14, "No Excuses, Many Reasons"). But these few children are not proof, precisely because they are exceptions. Poverty is not an excuse. It is a condition, like gravity, that affects virtually everything.

Poor children get off to a bad start before they're born. Their mothers are likely to get prenatal care late, if at all, which can impair the children's later intellectual functioning. These children are more than three times as likely as nonpoor children to have stunted growth. They are about twice as likely to have physical and mental disabilities, and are seven times more likely to be abused or neglected. And they are more than three times more likely to die. What these kids need are high standards, right?

Poverty stifles school performance. Researchers once examined the achievement of students in high- and low-poverty schools. They defined high-poverty schools as those with more than 75 percent of the students eligible for free and reduced-price lunches. Low-poverty schools had zero to 20 percent eligibility.

> Poverty stifles school performance.

The researchers first categorized kids in terms of the dominant letter grade on their report cards, then looked to see how the various categories fared on standardized tests of reading and math. On such tests, average is the 50th percentile. Students in low-poverty schools who took home "A's" scored at the 81st percentile in reading and at the 87th percentile in math. Students in high-poverty schools whose report cards said "A" scored higher than those who got lower grades, but they did not reach even the 40th percentile on either test.[2]

These research findings just put numbers on descriptions of poverty-ridden schools that have been around for a long time. In the 1960s, the education crisis of children in poverty was described in books—written by teachers—such as *Death at an Early Age*, *36 Children*, and *The Way It Spozed to Be*. In that era, people hoped and believed that Head Start and Title I would cure the problem. Jonathan Kozol, author of *Death at an Early*

Age, returned in 1991 with *Savage Inequalities* to tell us they haven't.

Researchers analyzing one international study concluded that if the United States sample had been made up of only affluent school districts, it would have placed second in math, the subject in which we are such putative dolts. If the American sample had come from poor districts, however, we would have landed at the bottom, near Nigeria and Swaziland.[3] These same researchers found that, among industrialized nations, the United States has by far the highest incidence of child poverty: 21.5 percent at the time, around 20 percent currently. No one else even came close. Australia had the second-highest poverty rate at 14 percent.

Given the devastating impact of poverty on school performance, and given the importance of schooling, one would think that a rich country such as the United States would make the elimination of poverty a high priority. But it isn't on anyone's agenda. The affluent eye (and the previously affluent eye) is watching the Dow Jones, not the poverty rate.

> One would think that a rich country such as the United States would make the elimination of poverty a high priority.

Instead of facing the problem head-on, people are creating a smoke screen, arguing that to cure the problems of poor schools we need vouchers that will permit poor kids to attend private schools. This is absurd. Most private schools are not about to accept large numbers of students who score as low as the lowest scoring nations, just as they do not accept students with limited English proficiency or students requiring special education services.

And, even under the most optimistic of assumptions, private schools could accommodate no more than 4 percent of the students currently enrolled in public schools. A decade ago, some free market types argued that if there were competition, new schools would spring up like gas stations and fast-food restaurants. They don't make that claim any more. Let's hope they have come to realize that creating a school with a comprehensive curriculum and a competent faculty is a tad bit more complicated than opening a Mclookalike burger-flipping joint.

So, unless we face the problem of poverty directly, it won't disappear. At the time this essay first appeared, I wrote, "But should

Mr. Bradley become president, he will have to deal with it using animals currently in short supply: politicians with spines." The ensuing four years have seen them decrease to become a truly endangered species.

Notes

1. George F. Will, "Shame, School Reform's Weak Weapon." *Washington Post,* March 2, 2003, p. B7.

2. Abt Associates, *Prospects.* Boston: Author, 1993.

3. Kevin J. Payne and Bruce J. Biddle, "Poor School Funding, Child Poverty and Mathematics Achievement." *Educational Researcher,* September, 1999, pp. 4–13.

10 April Foolishness
"A Nation At Risk" at Twenty

Twenty years ago this month, Ronald Reagan's chief of staff, Jim Baker, and Reagan adviser, Mike Deaver, defeated Reagan's attorney general, Ed Meese, in a battle of White House insiders. Over Meese's strong objections, they persuaded President Reagan to accept the report of the National Commission on Excellence in Education, "A Nation At Risk." Secretary of Education Terrel H. Bell, had convened the commission. In his memoir, *The Thirteenth Man*, Bell recalls that he sought a "Sputnik-type occurrence" that would dramatize all the "constant complaints about education and its effectiveness" that he kept hearing. Unable to produce such an event, Bell settled for a booklet with thirty-six pages of text and twenty-nine pages of appendices about who testified before the Commission or presented it with a paper.

Meese and his fellow conservatives hated "Risk" because it did not address any of Reagan's education agenda items: vouchers, tuition tax credits, restoring school prayer, and abolishing the U.S. Department of Education. Baker called those issues "extraneous and irrelevant." He and the moderates of the White House staff thought the report contained a lot of good stuff on which to campaign. They were more right than they knew. Bell's memoir notes that "Risk" stole the education issue from the Democratic candidate, Walter Mondale, and then served as a smoke screen to deflect attention from cuts in welfare, Medicaid, and other social programs.

Reagan accepted the report, but his speech acknowledging it largely ignored the report's content and simply reiterated his agenda. According to Bell, the talk was virtually identical to the speech that he had read and rejected the previous day. The *Washington Post* called it a "homily." Bell tells of looking around as Reagan spoke and noticing that "Ed Meese was standing there with a big smile on his face."

Despite Meese's sabotage, "Risk" played big in the media. In the month following the report's publication, the *Washington Post* carried no fewer than twenty-eight stories. Few were critical. Joseph Kraft did excoriate conservatives for using it to beat up on liberals without offering anything constructive. William F. Buckley chided it for recommendations that "you and I would come up with over the phone." *New York Times* columnist Russell Baker contended that a sentence containing a phrase like "a rising tide of mediocrity," "wouldn't be worth more than a C in tenth grade English." About the authors' writing overall, Baker said, "I'm giving them an A+ in mediocrity."

Any students who were in first grade when "Risk" appeared and who went directly from high school graduation into the work force have been there for eight years. Those who went on to bachelor's degrees have been on the job for four years. Despite the report's dire predictions of national collapse without immediate education reform, productivity has soared since these new workers arrived. What, then, are we to make of "A Nation At Risk" twenty years on?

The report's stentorian Cold Warrior rhetoric commanded and commands attention: "If an unfriendly foreign power had attempted to impose on America the mediocre educational performance that exists today, we might well have viewed it as an act of war." By contrast, the report's recommendations were, as Buckley and others observed, banal. They called for nothing new, only for more: more science, more mathematics, more computer science, more foreign language, more homework, more rigorous courses, more time on task, more hours in the school day, more days in the school year, more training for teachers, more money for teachers—hardly the stuff of revolution. And even those mundane recommendations were based on a set of risk allegations that Peter Applebome in the *New York Times* later called "skillful propaganda." Indeed, the report was a veritable golden treasury of slanted, spun, and distorted statistics.

Before actually listing the risk factors, "Risk" told America why those indicators meant we were in such danger. Stop worrying so much about the Red Menace, the booklet said. The threat was not that our enemies would bomb us off the planet, but that our friends, especially Germany, Japan, and Korea, would outsmart us and wrest away control of the world economy: "If only to keep and improve on the slim competitive edge we still retain in world markets, we must dedicate ourselves to the reform of our educational system." In penning this sentence, the Commissioners tightly yoked the nation's global competitiveness to how well our thirteen-year-olds bubbled in test answer sheets. This theory was, to be kind, without merit. A few, such as education historian Lawrence Cremin, saw the theory for the nonsense that it was. In *Popular Education and its Discontents,* Cremin wrote

> American economic competitiveness with Japan and other nations is to a considerable degree a function of monetary, trade, and industrial policy, and of decisions made by the President and Congress, the Federal Reserve Board, and the Federal Departments of the Treasury, Commerce and Labor. Therefore, to conclude that problems of international competitiveness can be solved by educational reform, especially educational reform defined solely as school reform, is not merely utopian and millenialist, it is at best a foolish and at worst a crass effort to direct attention away from those truly responsible for doing something about competitiveness and to lay the burden instead on the schools. It is a device that has been used repeatedly in the history of American education.[1]

Alas, Cremin's wisdom was read only by educators—and not by too many of them, either—not the policy makers who needed to absorb his message.

In fact, "Risk's" theory became very popular in the late 1980s when the nation slid into the recession that would cost George H. W. Bush a second term. One then heard many variations of "Lousy schools are producing a lousy workforce and that's killing us in the global marketplace." The economy, however, was not listening to the litany and came roaring back. By late 1993 and early 1994, headlines over stories about the economy expressed energy and confidence: "The American Economy: Back on Top" (*New York Times*), "America Cranks It Up," (*U.S. News & World Report*), and "Rising Sun Meets Rising Sam" (*Washington Post*).

Of course, it was *possible* that the comeback had actually been spurred by true and large improvements in the schools. It was at least as possible as that school improvements after *Sputnik* in 1957 had got us a man on the moon in 1969. If it were true, though, it was a national secret. In fact, the school critics denied that there had been any gains. Three months after the *Times* declared the American economy was again number one in the world, IBM CEO Lou Gerstner took to the *Times'* op-ed page to declare "Our Schools Are Broken." One reads Gerstner's essay in vain for any hint that schools are on the way up.

Indeed, evidence abounds that Gerstner and other school critics, especially in the first Bush administration, strove mightily to keep the report's dire warning alive—and so strive today. In 2001, Gerstner was back in both the *Post* and the *Times*. The CEOs of Intel, Texas Instruments, and State Farm Insurance all penned op-ed essays for national newspapers about the poor quality of schools, as did Secretary of Health and Human Services Tommy Thompson, former senator John Glenn, former governor of Delaware Pete DuPont, and former Secretary of Education William J. Bennett.

During the time of "Risk," they not only hyped alleged bad news, but also deliberately suppressed good news, or ignored it when they couldn't actually suppress it. The most egregious example of suppression, at least the most egregious we know about, was that of "The Sandia Report." Assembled in 1990 by engineers at Sandia National Laboratories in Albuquerque, the report presented seventy-eight pages of graphs and tables and seventy-eight pages of text to explain the graphs and tables. It concluded that while there were many problems in public education, there was no systemwide crisis. Secretary of Energy James Watkins, who had

> *The most egregious example of the federal government's suppression of reports favorable to education—that we know about—was that of "The Sandia Report."*

asked for the report, called it "dead wrong" in the *Albuquerque Journal*. Briefed by the Sandia engineers who compiled it, Deputy Secretary of Education and former Xerox CEO David Kearns told them, "You bury this or I'll bury you." The engineers were forbidden to leave New Mexico to discuss the report. Officially, according to Assistant Secretary of Education, Diane Ravitch, the report was undergoing "peer review" by other agencies (an unprecedented occurrence) and was not ready for publication. Sandia vice president Lee Bray supervised the engineers who produced the report. I asked Bray, now retired, about the report's fate. He affirmed it was definitely, deliberately suppressed.[2]

There were other instances of accentuating the negative. In February 1992, a small international comparison in mathematics and science appeared. America's ranks were largely but not entirely low, although actual scores were near the international averages. Secretary of Education Lamar Alexander and Assistant Secretary Ravitch held a press conference that garnered wide coverage in both print and electronic media. "An 'F' in World Competition," was *Newsweek*'s headline, *Newsweek* having fallen for the hokum that high test scores equal international competitiveness. The *Post* had Alexander saying the study's outcome was a "clear warning that even good schools are not properly preparing students for world competition."

Critics would hammer the schools with this international study for years. In January 1996, for instance, a full-page ad in the *New York Times* showed the rankings of fourteen-year-olds in math. Among fifteen countries, America was 14th. "If this were a ranking in Olympic hockey, we would be outraged," said a large-type ad (1996 was a summer Olympics year). The immediate source of the ad was the Ad Council, but the sponsors were, in the order in which they were listed in the ad, the Business Roundtable, the U.S. Department of Education, The National Governors' Association, the American Federation of Teachers, and the National Alliance of Business. Clearly, with friends like these, public schools needed no enemies.

Five months after the math–science study, another international comparison appeared, this one in reading. No one knew. *Education Week* (EW) discovered the study first, but only two months after the results were published and then only by accident. Robert Rothman, an EW reporter at the time, received a copy from a friend in Europe. American nine-year-olds ranked second in the world among twenty-seven nations. American fourteen-year-olds were eighth among thirty-one countries, but only Finland had a significantly higher score. EW ran the story on the front page. *USA Today* played off the EW account with its own page one piece. *USA Today*'s article included a quote from Deputy Assistant Secretary of Education Francie Alexander that reflected the Bush administration's handling of good news: She dismissed the study as irrelevant. (I was told by someone in Office of Educational Research and Improvement that Ravitch handed the results to a group of researchers in the Office and told the group to make the study disappear. The study was conducted by an educational organization based in The Hague, so, unlike the federally funded Sandia Report, it couldn't be suppressed. The group of researchers produced about six inches worth of reports but couldn't make the results go away.)

While "Risk" offered a litany of spun statistics about the risk we faced, its authors and fellow believers presented no actual *data* to support the contention that high test scores equal competitiveness except the most circumstantial. The arguments heard around the country typically went like this: "Asian nations have high test scores. Asian nations ["Asian Tigers," they were called then], especially Japan, have experienced economic miracles. Therefore, the high test scores produced the economic good times." The National Commission on Excellence in Education and many school critics made a mistake that no educated person should: They confused correlation with causality.

The "data" on education and competitiveness consisted largely of testimonials from Americans who visited Japanese schools. On returning from Japan, educational researcher, Herbert Walberg said many features of the Japanese system should be adopted here. "I think it's portable. Gumption and willpower, that's the key."[3] The believers overlooked cautionary tales such as Ken Schooland's *Shogun's Ghosts: The Dark Side of Japanese Education,* or the unpretty picture of Japanese schools presented in the education chapters of Karel van Wolferen's *The Enigma of Japanese Power.*

> The "data" on education and competitiveness consisted largely of testimonials from Americans who visited Japanese schools.

How representative were the Japanese schools these American visitors saw is not known, but, without doubt, they saw only the good side. I once asked Paul George at the University of Florida about gaining entrance to less than stellar Japanese schools. George has spent years in Japanese schools of various levels of achievement. His reply was succinct: "Look, there are 27 high schools in Osaka, ranked 1 to 27. You can easily get into the top few. You would have a much harder time getting into #12 or #13. Not even Japanese researchers can get into #27."

The proponents of the test score theory of economic health grew quiet after the Japanese discovered that the emperor's palace and grounds were actually *not* worth more than the entire state of California, a widely disseminated "fact" in Japan in the 80s. Japan has foundered economically now for twelve years. The government *admits* that bad loans from banks to corporations amount to more than 10 percent of its gross domestic product. Some estimate the size of the bad loans as high as 75 percent of GDP. We now see headlines such as "The Sinking Sun?" (*New York Times*) and "A Second Decade of Economic Woes?" (*Washington Post*).

The case of Japan presents a counter example to the idea that high test scores assure a thriving economy, but there is a more general method available to test the report's hypothesis high scores equal competitiveness. For this test I located thirty-five nations that had rankings in the Third International Mathematics and Science Study (TIMSS) eighth grade tests and also rankings for global competitiveness from the Geneva think tank, the World Economic Forum (WEF). Among these thirty-five the United States in 2001 was ranked number one. Among all seventy-five countries that the WEF ranked in its *Global Competitiveness Report 2001–2002*, America was #2, trailing Finland, but Finland did not take part in the first round of TIMSS in 1995. The rank order correlation coefficient between test scores and competitiveness was +.19, virtually zero. If five countries that scored low on both variables were removed from the list, the coefficient actually became negative.

"Risk" built its case for competitiveness out of whole cloth, but to make its case for the dire state of American education, it did provide a lot of statistics. It was the spin on these stats that led Applebome to characterize "Risk" as propaganda. Consider these:

- ■ "Over half the population of gifted students do not match their tested ability with comparable achievement."

I have asked both commissioners and staff to the commission where this statistic came from. No one knows. It makes no sense because twenty years ago, the principal instruments for identifying gifted kids were achievement tests.

- ■ "Average tested achievement of students graduating from college is also lower."

Another nonexistent statistic.

- ■ "There was a steady decline in science achievement scores of U.S. 17-year-olds as measured by national assessments of science in 1969, 1973 and 1977."

Maybe, maybe not. The National Assessment of Educational Progress (NAEP) was not originally designed to produce trends, and the scores for 1969 and 1973 are backward extrapolations from the 1977 assessment. In any case, the declines were smaller for nine- and thirteen-year-olds and had already been wiped out by gains on the 1982 assessment. Scores for reading and math for all three ages assessed by the NAEP were stable or inching up. The commissioners thus had nine trendlines (three ages: nine, thirteen, and seventeen; and three subjects, reading, math, and science), only one of which could be used to support crisis rhetoric. That was the only one they used.

- ■ "The College Board's Scholastic Aptitude Tests demonstrate a virtually unbroken decline from 1963 to 1980."

This was true, but the Board's own investigative panel described a complex trend to which many variables contributed. It ascribed most of the change to changes in who was taking the test—more minorities, more women, more students with mediocre high school records, more students from low-income families.

When the standards for the SAT were set, the students who received 500 as an average score were an elite: 10,654 high schoolers mostly living in New England. Ninety-eight percent were white, 61 percent were male, and 41 percent had attended private college preparatory high schools. In 1982, the year the report's commissioners labored, 988,270 seniors huddled in angst on Saturday mornings to bubble in SAT answer sheets. Eighty-four percent of these students were white, 52 percent were female, 44 percent had mothers with a high school diploma or less, 27 percent came from families with incomes under $18,000, and 81 percent attended public schools.

All of those demographic changes are associated with lower scores on any test. It would have been very suspicious if the scores had *not* declined.

- "Average achievement of high school students on most standardized tests is now lower than 26 years ago when Sputnik was launched."

The commissioners could not have known if this were true for "most standardized tests." At the time, most companies that produced standardized tests did not equate them from form to form over time. They used a "floating norm." Whenever they renormed their tests, whatever raw score corresponded to the 50th percentile became the new norm. Only the Iowa Tests of Basic Skills (ITBS, grades 3–8) and Iowa Tests of Educational Development (ITED, grades 9–12) were referenced to a fixed standard and equated from form to form, beginning in 1955. To examine test score trends over time, one needs a test referenced to a fixed standard by which each new form equates to the earlier form. Only the ITBS-ITED battery met this requirement.

It *was* true that on the ITED, scores were lower than when *Sputnik* was launched—barely. The commissioners could have noted that scores had risen for five consecutive years and that their statement about test scores and *Sputnik* didn't apply to most middle or elementary grades.

The five-year rise had been preceded by a decade-long decline that itself was preceded by a ten-year rise. Scores rose from 1955, a baseline year when the test was renormed and qualitatively changed as well, to about 1965. Scores then fell until about 1975, reversed, and climbed to *record high levels* by 1985 (something unnoticed by critics or media).

It is instructive to examine what the nation was experiencing during this ten years of falling test scores, from 1965 to 1975. The decade was anteceded by one year by the Civil Rights Act of 1964, then opened with the Watts riots in Los Angeles. Urban violence then spread across the nation. The decade contained Black Panthers, the Symbionese Liberation Army, Students for a Democratic Society, the Free Speech Movement, the Summer of Love, Woodstock, Altamont, Ken Kesey and his LSD-laced band of Merry Pranksters, the Kent State atrocities, and the 1968 Chicago Police Riot. Martin Luther King, Jr., Robert F. Kennedy, and Malcolm X were all assassinated. The country became obsessed with and depressed by first the war in Vietnam and then Watergate. "Recreational drugs"—pot, acid, speed, Quaaludes, amyl nitrate—had become popular. If you remember the Sixties, the saying goes, you weren't there. And don't trust anyone over thirty.

Popular books included anti-Establishment tracts such as *The Making of a Counter Culture*, *The Greening of America*, and *The Pursuit of Loneliness*. Books critical of schools included *Death at an Early Age*, *The Way It Spozed to Be*, *36 Children*, *Free Schools*, *Deschooling Society*, *The Death of School*, *How Children Fail*, *The Student as Nigger*, *Teaching as a Subversive Activity*, and, most influential, Charles Silberman's 1970 tome, *Crisis in the Classroom*.

Under these conditions of social upheaval centered in the schools and universities, it would have been a bloody *miracle* if test scores had *not* fallen. When "Risk" appeared, universities and education associations fell all over themselves lauding it. The education associations said that they welcomed the attention after a decade of neglect. "We are pleased education is back on the American agenda," wrote Paul Salmon, Executive Director of the American Association of School Administrators. The education associations also said, later, that they didn't want to appear defensive. They also said, much later and in private, that they were certain that with all these problems in education, the money would surely follow. They were wrong.

> *Under these conditions of social upheaval centered in the schools and universities, it would have been a bloody* miracle *if test scores had* not *fallen.*

As for the universities—well, a crisis in our schools always presents a great opportunity for educational researchers seeking to liberate money from foundations and governments. "A Nation At Risk" was to the research universities as September 11 was to the arms and security industries. As Susan Fuhrman, Dean of the School of Education at the University of Pennsylvania, once said at a meeting, "If you want money, ya gotta say the schools are lousy. So what else is new?"

The National Commission on Excellence in Education commissioned over forty papers that laid out the crisis. Virtually all of them were written by academics. The Commission acknowledged only one that was written by someone actually working in a school and it was not a commissioned work. Harvey Prokop, a teacher in San Diego, wrote a critique of a Commission seminar in his town, *The Student's Role in Learning*.

Alas, nothing else is new, and indeed, we must recognize that good news about public schools serves no one's political education reform agenda even if it does make teachers, kids, parents, and administrators feel a little better. Conservatives want vouchers and tuition tax credits; liberals want more resources for schools; free marketers want to privatize the schools and make money; fundamentalists want to teach religion and not worry about the First Amendment; Catholic schools want to stanch their student hemorrhage (and create more Catholics); home schooling advocates want just that; and various other groups no doubt just want to be with their "own kind." All groups believe they improve their chances of getting what they variously want if they pummel the public schools.

> *Good news about public schools serves no one's political education reform agenda even if it makes teachers, kids, parents, and administrators feel a little better.*

It has, though, been twenty years since "A Nation At Risk" appeared. It is clear that "Risk" was false then and is false now. Today, the laments are old and tired—and still false. "Test Scores Lag as School Spending Soars" heralds the headline of a 2002 press release from the American Legislative Exchange Council. Ho-hum. The various education special interest groups need another treatise to rally round. They have one. It's called No Child Left Behind. It's a weapon of mass destruction, and the target is the public school system. Today, our public schools are truly at risk.

Notes

1. Lawrence J. Cremin. 1989. *Popular Education and Its Discontents.* New York: Harper & Row.

2. The report finally appeared in 1993 as the entirety of the May/June 1993 issue of the *Journal of Educational Research* under the title, "Perspectives on Education in America."

3. Keith Richburg. "Japanese Education: Admired but Not Easily Imported." *Washington Post,* October 19, 1985, p. A1.

What If "Failing Schools" Aren't?
Or, What I Did Last Summer

A few years ago, the *Baltimore Sun* ran a story under the headline "Pupils Lose Ground in City Schools: The Longer They
Stay in the System, the More They Fall Behind." You might
have seen something similar in other big-city papers. The headline and the story imply that the schools are failing the children.
There is now considerable evidence that it might not be the
schools that are failing.

The largest and most tightly controlled study to bear on "losing ground" was conducted by researchers at Johns Hopkins
University.[1] They tracked children for five years, administering
tests in the fall and spring of each year. Poor children entered
school behind their middle-class and affluent peers. And as they
navigated through the elementary grades, they fell farther and farther beyond, just as the headline said.

But because the researchers gave tests in the spring and again
when the children returned to school in the fall, they could get a
read on what happened over the sum-
mer months. The poor kids lost
ground. Middle-class children held
their own in math and gained in reading. Affluent kids gained in both sub-

*The poor kids lost ground.
Affluent kids gained in both
math and reading.*

jects. The gains were small compared with the gains seen during the school years (which should be a great relief to educators), but they were there.

When the researchers looked at test score changes from fall to spring, they found that the poor kids gained as much as their middle-class and affluent peers. It is thus rather hard to make the case that it is the schools that are failing, although someone appears to make that case most every day. Another set of researchers concluded that "the differential progress made during the four summers between second and sixth grade accounts for upwards of 80 percent of the achievement difference between economically advantaged and ghetto schools."[2]

Now, the No Child Left Behind Act of 2001 requires schools to make adequate yearly progress (AYP) on tests of reading and mathematics and, in a couple of years, science. But if low-income and middle-class schools show the same amount of progress during the school year, but kids in low-income schools lose much of those gains over the summer, then low-income schools will be labeled failing when they aren't.

As noted, the gains that show up in middle-class and affluent kids over the summer are quite small compared with those seen during the school year. You are probably not surprised at this, but it is an important datum. A 1966 study that came to be widely known as "the Coleman Report" was often cited as showing that "schools don't matter."[3] It didn't show that, and Coleman never claimed it did but how it was often reported. The Hopkins study clearly shows the following:

> *Schools do matter, and they matter the most when support for academic learning outside school is weak.*

Schools do matter, and they matter the most when support for academic learning outside school is weak. . . . The powerful role of school in fostering the achievement of all children is one lesson informed by a seasonal perspective on learning. A second is that disadvantaged children, on the whole, are capable learners. They keep up during the school year, but before they start first grade and in summers between grades, the out-of-school resources available to them are not sufficient to support their achievement. When our study group started school, their pre-reading and pre-math skills reflected their uneven family situations, and these initial differences were magnified across the primary grades because of the summer setback *despite the equalizing effect of their school experiences.* (emphasis in the original, 183)

The researchers recommended summer school for poor children, but they quickly pointed out that the summer gains seen in middle-class kids took place out of the school setting: "We found that better-off children in the study more often went to city and state parks, fairs, or carnivals, and took day or overnight trips. They also took swimming, dance, and music lessons; visited parks, museums, science centers, and zoos; and more often went to the library in summer." They also played more organized games, which are useful in teaching rules, teamwork, sequences, and even some mathematics—it's sixty feet to first base in softball, and so on.

This is to say that the "summer school" for poor kids need not necessarily be a repeat of the school year or, worse, dreary drill-and-kill worksheets. The summer activities of the better-off kids look very much like those encompassed by the term *enrichment*.

Impoverished communities are at a disadvantage in providing material to learners. They get most of their reading materials from school libraries, and these have older, smaller, and less diverse collections than those found in more affluent communities. And, even if the school is open for summer programs, the library is often locked. Affluent communities have three times as many stores selling children's books as do poor communities, and the number of titles in affluent stores exceeds, and sometimes far exceeds, the number of titles in stores in poor areas.

> *Even if the school is open for summer programs, the library is often locked.*

This study did not examine family issues in achievement, but others have. One typical study, for instance, observed mothers from professional families and mothers who were on welfare as they interacted with their three-year-old children. The three-year-old *children* of professional mothers used more words than did the mothers on welfare during these interactions. Interactions between mother and child in poverty settings were much more likely to be characterized by negative emotions.[4] Another study found parents with a professional-level education speaking to their children at 2,200 words, compared with 1,300 words per hour for blue-collar parents and only 600 words per hour for welfare families. The study made no attempt to measure the complexity of the utterances.[5]

Although results like these have been embraced by people who advocate (and make money from) year-round schooling, politicians and policy makers in general don't seem to want to come to terms with the implications. I published an article on summer loss on the op-ed page of the *Washington Post* and got only a couple of letters and emails and a few phone calls in response. Princeton economist Alan Krueger wrote a similar article for the *New York Times* that got more attention, but nothing that spilled over into policy or program changes.

This is too bad, because not only will schools be blamed for something that is not their fault, but in general the failure to attend to summer loss puts more focus on what goes on in schools to the exclusion of everything else. Others have noticed this:

> We have placed too much confidence in school reforms that affected only six hours a day of a child's life . . . In the face of many negative influences on our children that come from outside the school, we have done well to maintain our high school completion rate and our level of performance on achievement measures. . . . We have foolishly concluded that any problems with the levels of academic achievement have been caused by faulty schools staffed by inept teachers. School leaders and others must turn increasingly to parents, homes, and communities.

Unfortunately, the person who penned these words had this epiphany too late. Terrel Bell wrote them in 1993.[6] Ten years earlier, as Secretary of Education, Bell had put together the commission that produced the little blue book of propaganda that focused attention on the alleged failures of the schools, "A Nation At Risk" (see Chapter 10 "April Foolishness: 'A Nation At Risk' at Twenty").

Notes

1. Karl Alexander, Doris Entwisle, and Linda Olson, "Schools, Inequality and Achievement: A Seasonal Perspective." *Educational Evaluation and Policy Analysis,* Summer, 2001.

2. Cited in Richard F. Allington and Anne McGill-Franzen, "The Impact of Summer Loss on Reading Achievement," available from Allington at ra@coe.ufl.edu.

3. Coleman, James, Ernest P. Campbell, Carol J. Hobson, James McPartland, Alexander M. Mood, Frederic D. Weinfeld, and Robert L. York, *Equality of Educational Opportunity.* Washington, DC: U.S. Government Printing Office, 1966.

4. Betty Hart and Todd R. Risley, *Meaningful Differences.* Baltimore: Paul H. Brookes, 1995.

5. Cited in Richard Rothstein, *The Way We Were?* New York: The Century Foundation, 1998.

6. Terrell Bell, "Reflections One Decade after 'A Nation At Risk.'" *Phi Delta Kappan,* April, 1993, pp. 592–97.

12 Getting Dumber in School?

This essay first appeared in the March 2001 issue of *Principal Leadership*. It debunks the myth that the longer kids stay in school, the dumber they get relative to their foreign peers. A bit of the discussion at the end concentrates on the implications of the article for principals, but teachers should find most of it cogent as well. In fact, it might explain why some teachers find their principals know so little about curriculum and instruction.

On December 5, 2000, the U.S. Department of Education released the results of TIMSS-R (Third International Mathematics and Science Study–Repeat). On December 8, 2000, IBM CEO Louis V. Gerstner and Wisconsin Governor Tommy G. Thompson published their take on the results in an op-ed in the *New York Times*. They wrote, "The message here is extraordinary and irrefutable: Every day our public schools are open, the gulf between our children and the world's top performers grows wider."

This is not the first time Gerstner has assailed math and science "declines" in this country. At a 1999 education "summit" he referred to TIMSS results as showing the good (fourth grade), the bad (eighth grade), and the ugly (twelfth grade) about U.S.

schools (Gerstner 1999). Former Secretary of Education William J. Bennett seems to agree. At a meeting honoring the 25th anniversary of the Heritage Foundation, he chimed in, "In America today, the longer kids stay in school the dumber they get relative to students in other industrialized countries" (Bennett 2000). This is quite an indictment. Does it hold up under scrutiny? Only in part. The basic facts are these: In TIMSS-O (for "Original"), U.S. students were near the top as fourth graders, in the middle as eighth graders, and apparently near the bottom as seniors. *Apparently* is the operative word. The decline from grade 4 to grade 8 probably is real; the decline from grade 8 to grade 12 probably is not.

In TIMSS-R, which tested only eighth graders, U.S. students were more above average than in TIMSS-O, but some said this was because many of the countries added to the study were not developed nations. These countries did boost U.S. rankings. However, thirteen countries of the forty-one in TIMSS-O did not take part in TIMSS-R. Of these, five had scored significantly higher than the United States, six had scored significantly lower, and two had scores similar to those of the United States. If one assumes that these countries would have performed similarly in TIMSS-R had they taken part, then a TIMSS-R made up of the original forty-one countries would have produced the same results: U.S. students would have finished smack in the middle.

Some U.S. students in grade 4 during TIMSS-O were tested in grade 8 for TIMSS-R. When compared with students in the seventeen nations that participated in grade 4 in TIMSS-O and grade 8 in TIMSS-R, they, too, had lost ground and scored around the average.

Finally, among the facts of the case are some that were lost for almost a decade. An international study of reading skills found that U.S. students were outscored only by Finland at both ages tested—9 and 14. Also at both ages tested, the best readers in the United States outscored the best readers of the thirty other nations involved (Elley 1992). More about these data and their disappearance later.

Among the possible factors contributing to a decline in math and science between grades 4 and 8, two stand out: the size of textbooks and the traditional view U.S. educators have of the middle school years.

First, let's look at our textbooks. Unlike other nations that have centralized, government-determined texts, our textbooks are developed in the private sector. The consequences of this are significant. In other countries, there is no "market" for textbooks. Here, textbook publishers want to sell to the widest possible market. If they limit themselves to a single approach, they will lose by default in those parts of the market using a different approach.

The result is a kitchen-sink process of constructing textbooks with one eye on the market—especially the big adoption states, Texas and California. This approach produces what Harriet Tyson-Bernstein calls "mentioning": "Books accused of 'mentioning' are long on facts and terms but short on ideas and explanations" (1988, 27). They flit from factoid to factoid, lacking any context or structure.

TIMSS analyses of how many topics U.S. and foreign teachers cover show the Americans roaming over many more topics than those in other countries. Teachers, driven by the tyranny of scope and sequence, try to cover it all. Such coverage is of necessity often too brief and too shallow.

Teachers, driven by the tyranny of scope and sequence, try to cover it all.

More recent studies suggest that, unfortunately, U.S. teachers do not have sufficient understanding about mathematics to render some coherence from the inchoate texts. U.S. teachers concentrate on procedures and algorithms (Stigler and Hiebert 1999; Ma 1999). They view mathematics as a set of skills they need to impart to students. In at least some other nations, the approach is more conceptual.

The other factor in the grades 4 to 8 decline is that U.S. educators typically view the middle grades as the culmination of elementary school. And although recent reform efforts encourage increased academic rigor, some middle school teachers view these years more as a period in which to emphasize identity and self-esteem, not academics. In other nations, these grades are seen as the start of the more intense academic study of secondary school. We look backward and review past material; other countries look forward and introduce new material. Thus, we find Japanese students receiving substantial amounts of algebra in seventh grade and geometry in eighth.

As for the decline from grade 8 to grade 12, it probably doesn't exist. I say "probably" because the TIMSS final year study is such a morass of bad data it's impossible to draw any firm conclusions. But that hasn't stopped people from trying. The final year study entered the popular culture as showing that our twelfth graders went up against their twelfth graders and got stomped and that our best twelfth graders went up against their best twelfth graders and got stomped. That isn't what happened at all.

The official report is titled Mathematics and Science Achievement in the Final Year of Secondary School. For the United States, the "final year" is grade 12. For some other countries it is grade 13 or 14. In one country, the students tested were as old as U.S. college seniors.

The age differences reflect the different structures of secondary schools in different countries. After eighth grade, most U.S. students enter comprehensive high schools. In other nations, they enroll in schools with specialized curricula. In some countries, more than 50 percent of the students enter vocational programs. Others get five years of focused training in science and technology or the humanities. Comparisons across these different structures are iffy at best.

Cultural variables also affect the results. For instance, in most nations, teenagers are either students or workers, not both. In the final year study of TIMSS, though, 27 percent of U.S. seniors said that they worked twenty-one to thirty-five hours a week, and 28 percent said they worked more than thirty-five hours a week. No other country came close to these figures. Canada was second highest with 23 percent of its seniors saying they worked twenty-one to thirty-five hours a week, and 16 percent stating they worked more than thirty-five hours a week.

In the United States, the relationship between working and school performance is usually found to be curvilinear. A recent article indicated that students who work fifteen hours a week or less do better in school than those who work longer hours or those who don't work at all (Hine 2000). This relationship is illustrated in the U.S. scores in the TIMSS final year study. Students who worked up to fourteen hours a week scored higher than those who didn't work or those who worked more. In fact, their score was right at the international average, the same place as it was for the eighth graders. Those seniors who worked twenty-one to thirty-five hours a week scored considerably lower, and those who worked more than thirty-five hours a week were almost off the chart in terms of low scores. In fact, they outscored only South Africa. (Technically, they scored two points higher than next-to-last Cyprus, but the difference is too small to be statistically significant.)

The final year study was also afflicted by severe sampling problems. Only five nations met the study's own criteria for valid data. Russia tested only Russian-speaking students; Italy lopped off whole provinces. One wonders why the study was published at all. A possible answer lies in the fact that U.S. taxpayers ponied up $51 million for it.

A particular sampling problem was introduced by the inclusion of U.S. students in pre-calculus classes. This is problematic because 23 percent of the items in the advanced math test presumed that the test taker had taken calculus. TIMSS officials told me they tested these students "just to see how they'd do." Well, they did awful. They scored 100 points below U.S. students who actually had calculus under their academic belts. Those students who had actually taken calculus scored at the international average, just as students had as eighth graders.

> TIMSS said they tested these students on calculus "just to see how they'd do." Well, they did awful.

A smaller percentage of U.S. students take calculus than in many other countries because of decisions made during the reform efforts that followed the launch of *Sputnik* in 1957. Educators then decided that, for most students, calculus was a college-level course. That decision needs to be rethought.

What About Reading?

If you read only the op-ed pages of U.S. newspapers, you would think that mathematics and science are the only subjects schools teach, or at least the only important ones. But if you look into U.S. elementary school classrooms, you find teachers giving more time to the development of reading skills than to math and science combined.

It comes as no surprise, then, that U.S. students have always done well in international comparisons of reading. In the most recent study, U.S. nine-year-olds were second in the world among twenty-seven nations, and U.S. fourteen-year-olds eighth among thirty-one nations (Elley 1992). At both ages, only one nation, Finland, significantly outscored the United States. At both ages, the 90th, 95th, and 99th percentiles of U.S. students were the highest in the world. That is, our best readers outscored the best readers in all other countries (NCES 1994).

It says a lot about the politics of U.S. education that virtually no one knows about the study *How in the World Do Students Read?* It was conducted under the auspices of the International Association for the Evaluation of Educational Achievement (IEA), the same organization that oversaw TIMSS, and released in 1992. Why was it kept under wraps?

Recall that Ronald Reagan entered the White House in 1981 with an education agenda of restoring school prayer, eliminating the federal department of education, and establishing school vouchers and tuition tax credits. One strategy in the push for vouchers appears to have been to never say anything positive about U.S. schools. The shameful suppression of "The Sandia Report" is perhaps the best-known act in this strategy. George Bush pushed vouchers with even more enthusiasm than Reagan.

How this strategy played out in terms of international comparisons can be seen in the differential treatment of *How in the World Do Students Read?* and two other international studies that appeared just a few months earlier: *Learning Mathematics* and *Learning Science* (Lapointe, Mead, and Askew 1992; Lapointe, Askew, and Mead 1992). When the Educational Testing Service published these two studies in February 1992, the Department of Education held a press conference and the studies received broad attention from both print and electronic media. "An 'F' in World Competition" was the headline over the February 1992 *Newsweek* story. Although U.S. nine-year-olds had finished third in the world in science, U.S. fourteen-year-olds were near the bottom. Both ages were near the bottom in mathematics.

The IEA reading study appeared five months later, in July 1992. There was no press conference. There was no media coverage. Even education's "newspaper of record," *Education Week*, found out about the study by accident when a Europe-dwelling friend of then–*Education Week* reporter Robert Rothman sent him a copy from Germany.

Education Week naturally carried the story on page 1 (Rothman 1992). *USA Today* was the only daily paper to play off the *Education Week* story with its own front page, above-the-fold article (Manning 1992) in which then–Deputy Assistant Secretary of Education Francie Alexander dismissed the study. Four years later, Secretary of Education Richard Riley rereleased the results. *USA Today* dutifully carried it again on the front page. The story appeared in the *Los Angeles Times* and in a number of other papers.

The fact that U.S. nine-year-olds were second in reading while U.S. fourteen-year-olds were eighth might be taken as further support for the "getting dumber" contention. I don't think that holds in this instance when we look at the actual performance of the countries. In every race, someone will rank last, but that does not mean they don't perform well. The Olympic athlete who crosses the finish line last in the 100-meter dash is still the eighth fastest human being on the planet that day.

In the reading study, the top-ranked Finnish nine-year-olds had a score of 569 while U.S. kids scored 22 points lower at 547 (the scale is the same as the SAT's). At the fourteen-year-old level, Finnish students scored 560 and U.S. students 535, or 25 points below the Finns.

In terms of actual performance, the fourteen-year-olds scored as close to first place as the nine-year-olds. But at the older age level, the top-ranked countries were much more tightly bunched. In fact, the countries did not significantly differ from the U.S. score all the way from second-place France to 16th-ranked West Germany (still divided at the time the data were actually collected). Only Finland had a statistically significantly higher score.

At both ages, the U.S. 90th, 95th, and 99th percentiles were the highest in the world. The best U.S. readers outscored everyone else's best readers.

The 1992 study was not a fluke. American kids have done well on international reading comparisons dating back to the sixties. The most recent international study of reading, released in April, 2003, found Americans overall ninth among thirty-five nations. Only three countries, however, had scores that were significantly high than that garnered by American students.

Creating Questions and Change:
Principals in an Uncomfortable Position

What should principals do about the issues raised by the TIMSS-O and TIMSS-R findings? How administrators can deal with the textbook-size issue depends on their state or district's textbook adoption policy. And their ability to initiate curricular changes is likely to cause anxiety, although they are formally designated the instructional leaders for their buildings.

In 1962, Callahan found that the model for the principal was the business manager. In the years since his classic treatise, the influence of the private sector on schools has increased. Over and over, one hears that schools should incorporate the efficiencies of private business and industry, although what those efficiencies are is never clearly spelled out.

Tanner (2000) reports, "Today more than ever, textbooks on school administration focus on organizational theory and leadership modeled on the business world." In Tanner's state of New Jersey, the certification of principals "requires a host of courses in administration but not a single course in curriculum" (193). Tanner finds this perplexing because "the principal, being the administrator closest to the classroom teacher, is in the most critical position as Cremin pointed out, 'to look at the curriculum whole and raise insistent questions of priority and relationship'" (193).

It would seem that the TIMSS-O and TIMSS-R results should lead principals to ask "insistent questions" about what is taught when, what an appropriate sequence of study should look like, and how to extract a coherent mathematics curriculum from overly fat textbooks. Principals might want to use the TIMSS results to continue the discussion about how academics should be treated in the middle school grades.

Asking these questions might or might not lead to change—the consequences of our current math and science performance are hardly all negative. We have a glut of highly skilled people in all but a few select areas of information technology. Our economy, although slowing, has been robust for many years, and the expansion has been driven largely by the "mediocrities" described in 1983's "A Nation At Risk" (students in high school when "Risk" was published are now between the ages of thirty-one and thirty-six). Japanese students, on the other hand, consistently score at or near the top in international comparisons of math and science, yet their nation has been mired in stagnation and recession for thirteen years.

My sense, though, from looking at much data, is that math at least, and perhaps science, too, are not well presented in the nation's curricula, nor are they well taught. The studies by Stigler and Hiebert (1999) and especially by Ma (1999) are depressing in this regard. Some of the "insistent questions" should focus on why, and what we can do about it.

Works Cited

Bennett, W. J. 2000. "The State and Future of American Education." Available at www.heritage.org

Callahan, R. E. 1962. *Education and the Cult of Efficiency*. Chicago: University of Chicago Press.

Elley, W. P. 1992. *How in the World Do Students Read?* The Hague: International Association for the Evaluation of Educational Achievement. Available in this country through the International Reading Association, Newark, DE.

Gerstner, L. V., Jr. 1999. Keynote address given at the Education Summit in Palisades, New York. Available at www.ibm.com /lvg/speeches.phtml.

Hine, T. 2000. "Working at 14 and Paying for It." *Washington Post*, November 25, B5.

Lapointe, A. E., N. A. Mead, and J. M. Askew. 1992. *Learning Mathematics*. Princeton, NJ: Educational Testing Service.

Lapointe, A. E., J. M. Askew, and N. A. Mead. 1992. *Learning Science*. Princeton, NJ: Educational Testing Service.

Ma, L. 1999. *Knowing and Teaching Elementary Mathematics*. Mahwah, NJ: Lawrence Erlbaum.

Manning, A. 1992. "U.S. Kids Near Top of Class in Reading." *USA Today,* September 29, AI.

National Center for Education Statistics (NCES). 1994. The condition of education 1994, Supplemental Tables 16–3 and 16–4. Washington, DC: NCES.

Newsweek. 1992. "An 'F' in World Competition." *Newsweek,* February, 57.

Rothman, R. 1992. "U.S. Ranks High in International Study of Reading." *Education Week,* September 29, Al.

Stigler, J. W., and J. Hiebert. 1999. *The Teaching Gap.* New York: Free Press.

Tanner, D. 2000. "Manufacturing Problems and Selling Solutions: How to Succeed in the Education Business Without Really Educating." *Phi Delta Kappan* (November): 188–202.

Tyson-Bernstein, H. 1988. *A Conspiracy of Good Intentions: America's Textbook Fiasco.* Washington, DC: Council for Basic Education.

U.S. Department of Education. 1995. *Third International Mathematics and Science Study.* Washington, DC: USDOE.

———. 1999. *Third International Mathematics and Science Study–Repeat.* Washington, DC: USDOE.

13 International Comparisons
An Excuse to Avoid Meaningful
Educational Reform

A dd to the list of international comparisons that won't lead to significant or appropriate education reform the Program for International Student Assessment, or PISA. And that is too bad, because it could. First the facts: Conducted by the Organization for Economic Cooperation and Development (OECD), PISA tested fifteen-year-olds in twenty-eight OECD nations and four other countries: Brazil, Latvia, Liechtenstein, and the Russian Federation.

On the surface, the news from PISA is ho-hum. On tests of reading "literacy," mathematics "literacy," and science "literacy," American students were strictly average among the OECD nations, and slightly better than average with the four other countries included. (The OECD affixed the word *literacy* in an attempt to convey that the tests did not measure the students' mastery of school subjects, but their capacity to apply that knowledge to "real life" problems.)

According to the *New York Times*, U.S. Secretary of Education Rod Paige greeted the results with "dismay."[1] The press release from the Department of Education quoted Mr. Paige as saying, "Unfortunately, we are average across the board compared to other industrialized nations. In the global economy, these countries are our competitors. Average is not good enough for American kids."

Secretary Paige thus invoked the demonstrably false link between a nation's economic health and its kids' test-taking skills. An analysis of why that link is bogus is another essay, but we can note here that on July 10, 2001, the nation that consistently outscores all others, Singapore, declared its economy in recession. We can observe as well that despite its very high test scores, Japan has lain mired in recession for thirteen years and shows no sign of recovery.

International comparisons not only bring forth silly statements about test scores and the economy, they evoke howls of woe and outrage, claiming the studies show that the American educational system has failed. When PISA's predecessor, the Third International Mathematics and Science Study, or TIMSS, appeared, former Assistant U.S. Secretary of Education Chester E. Finn, Jr., took to the op-ed page of the *Wall Street Journal* to declare, "The public school system as we know it has proved that it cannot reform itself. It is an ossified government monopoly that functions largely for the benefit of its employees and interest groups rather than that of children and taxpayers."

> *International comparisons not only bring forth silly statements about test scores and the economy, they evoke howls of woe and outrage.*

Mr. Paige and Mr. Finn thus missed the singularly important finding of PISA and TIMSS: We don't have a "public school system as we know it." We have two. One is for poor and minority students; the other is for the rest of us. Of course, if they had noticed this, they might have been forced to take meaningful action. If Mr. Paige and Mr. Finn had asked, "How do the scores of the various ethnic groups rank them among the nations in PISA?" they would have seen the answer in the following table, giving "Ranks of American Ethnic Groups":

	Reading	Math	Science
White students	2nd	7th	4th
Black Students	26/29th	27/30th	27/30th
Hispanic students	26/29th	27/30th	27/30th

For blacks and Hispanics, the first rank is among the twenty-eight OECD nations; the second includes the other four countries. Asians do not constitute a large enough sample to generate a separate score. TIMSS produced an almost identical table.

To render the conditions of what I will call the Poor People's Education System more vivid and concrete, consider these vignettes:

- Classes in which teachers encourage students to bring boom boxes and headphones from home to drown out the noise from nearby machines.
- Schools with limited language, science, and mathematics offerings and no laboratories for any of the three subjects.
- Schools with obsolete textbooks or too few textbooks to assign homework.
- Schools with no guidance or support staff and pupil–teacher ratios of 43 to 1.
- Schools where termites have eaten through books, shelves, and school records and where condemned septic tanks form large dark spots on the playgrounds, where the kids play anyway.
- Young children picking up beer bottles, condoms, and bullets on school grounds. Officials take children out of reading instruction to perform this "beautification work."
- Rats scurrying about bread racks in cafeterias or running in dining areas with fruit in their mouths.
- Chemistry labs with no chemicals. Literature classes with no books. Computer classes in which, as one student puts it, "We sit there and talk about what we would be doing if we had computers."
- Classes with no teachers. A parade of substitutes shows movies.
- Students forced to stand or sit on windowsills until enough leave to have chairs for all.

The first five of these examples come from a 1990 legal brief filed in Alabama. But before you cluck your tongue over yet more travesties in the intractable Deep South, consider that the second five examples come from a class action in California filed in 2001. On the other hand, forty parents in Montgomery County, Maryland, recently coughed up $200,000 from their own pockets to ensure that renovations of a public elementary school would, according to news reports, "fit in with the upscale surrounding community."

We can immediately lay hands on $40 billion to rebuild after September 11, and another $15 billion to "bail out" the airlines (among the most profitable industries in the 1990s).[2] We are on the verge of not only repealing the corporate alternative minimum tax, but also of giving companies such as IBM, the Ford Motor Company, General Electric, and General Motors rebates of taxes already collected. In 2000, IBM reported $5.7 billion in pretax U.S. profits, but even with the alternative minimum tax paid only 3.4 percent in taxes. Ford reported $9.4 billion and paid 6.3 percent; General Electric reported $21.3 billion and paid 8.8 percent; and General Motors reported $2.9 billion in profits and got a $105 million rebate. From 1994 to 2000, GM reported $22.4 billion in profits and paid zero taxes. In spite of this largesse to corporations, somehow we can't find enough money to drive the rats and termites out of poverty-ridden schools.

> *In spite of this largesse to corporations, somehow we can't find enough money to drive the rats and termites out of poverty-ridden schools.*

As long as these scandalous conditions persist, what are we to make of slogans like "Don't throw money at the schools," "All children can learn," "We must hold all children to high standards," or "No child left behind"? They are hypocritical blather, no more.

Advocates of high standards and high-stakes testing have described them as engines for social justice. They are instead infernal machines of social destruction, exacerbating the achievement gap between rich and poor (see "The Governors' Debacle: The High-Stakes Testing Movement," Chapter 3). For instance, in Virginia, after four years of taking state-developed tests, pass rates on subjects like Algebra 1 remain below 10 percent in some city schools. In the adjoining suburbs, the pass rates are 75 percent and up. Kids will soon have to pass these tests to graduate from high school. Then, poor and minority kids in Virginia and in other states will roam the streets without diplomas, unemployable.

The conditions today bring to mind the 1970 words of Robert Coles in his remarkable series, *Children of Crisis:* "There are moments, and I believe this is one of them, when, whoever we are, observers or no, we have to throw up our hands in heaviness of heart and dismay and disgust and say, in desperation: God save them, those children, and for allowing such a state of affairs to continue, God save us, too." We didn't do anything meaningful then, either.

Notes

1. Diana Jean Schemo, "U.S. Students Are Middling on Test Given to 32 Nations." *New York Times,* December 5, 2001, p. A25.

2. As this is written, the estimated costs for a war against Iraq run from $60 billion to $200 billion. The Congressional Budget Office (CBO) two years ago projected a ten-year surplus of $5.6 trillion. It now projects a ten-year deficit of $1.6 trillion. Most commentators call the CBO estimate conservative and think it more like $3.2 trillion. Somehow the Bush administration will cut taxes even more, yet find the money to "rebuild" Iraq, but not the money to rebuild the crumbling schools, much less stock them with current textbooks.

14! No Excuses, Many Reasons
A Critique of the Heritage Foundation's "No Excuses" Report

I n recent years it has become popular at conservative think tanks
and among conservatives generally to find high-poverty, high-
minority schools that also have high test scores.[1] Once found,
these schools are held up as proof that most public schools are
failing. If these schools can do it, the argument goes, all schools
can. Poverty is not an excuse. On close examination, some of the
data collected are clearly spurious. Some of the test scores are
impossibly high. More of the schools, though, are exceptional in
many ways that cannot be generalized to all schools. As the
founder of one group of such schools, KIPP Academy, says, "You'd
need a whole pool of educators that does not exist today."

The article that follows analyzes one of the most widely disseminated studies, "No Excuses," published by the Heritage
Foundation. Michael Kinsley of *Slate* online magazine has characterized the Heritage Foundation as "a conservative propaganda
machine masquerading as a think tank." That strikes me as dead-
on accurate.

A slightly different version of this analysis was co-authored
with Bruce Biddle at the University of Missouri and disseminated
by the Education Policy Research Unit at Arizona State University
in July 2000.

"No Excuses: Lessons from 21 High-Performing, High-Poverty Schools" is a report by Samuel Casey Carter, a doctoral student in philosophy at Catholic University of America. Carter wrote it as a Bradley Foundation Fellow at the Heritage Foundation, which published it (Bradley is also a champion of Right-wing causes).

The report attempts to show that schools in impoverished areas do not need more resources, because the twenty-one "high-performing" schools described in the report purportedly make do with the resources of other public schools. (In some instances, this is not true—they have access to *more* resources). Early on, the report issues a disclaimer that it is not a formal research study. Indeed, the Bush administration, accepting only "scientifically based research," would quickly round-file it. It is research by anecdote, with inference by innuendo, and it fails to identify some of the factors that contribute to success in the schools it describes.

The report begins with a set of common traits purportedly extracted from the study, followed by a list of effective practices. The bulk of the report consists of short vignettes of the twenty-one schools involved.

The Traits

1. Principals must be free. They must have the freedom to establish curricula, hire and fire staff, and determine the schools' teaching style.
2. Principals use measurable goals to establish a culture of achievement.
3. Master teachers bring out the best in a faculty.
4. Rigorous and regular testing leads to continuous student achievement.
5. Achievement is the key to discipline.
6. Principals work actively with parents to make the home a center of learning.
7. Effort creates ability.

The report provides no information on how these traits were extracted. For instance, it mentions "master teachers" in only one of the twenty-one portraits of the schools. Another school deliberately hires uncertified teachers, and at another, teachers seem little more than acolytes of the principal.

Methodology

The failure of the report to provide information on the derivation of the traits is not surprising once one looks at Appendix D, "Definitions, Methods, and Procedure," which begins, "The findings reported here are not the product of formal scientific research."

The search for schools was anything but systematic: "After consulting with state education chiefs, their offices of assessment, state and local think tanks, teachers' unions, not-for-profit organizations supporting research in elementary and secondary education, family foundations providing financial support to outstanding high-poverty schools, educational consultants, and research organizations developing intervention programs for 'at-risk' students, a list of just over 400 prospective schools was assembled" (115).

Even some of the data in the report itself raise eyebrows. The Marva Collins School in Chicago reports that 70 percent of its students are low income, yet charges $4,500 a year in tuition and grants few scholarships. Marcus Garvey School in Los Angeles reports that "some students drive 30 to 40 miles each way to come to school." One can only cast a jaundiced eye whether students who have such ready access to automobiles and the money to afford such long distances fall into the category of low income.

Carter winnowed the list to "125 schools with very high concentrations of low-income students and a certain reputation for academic excellence." Some of these schools did not want to participate, and some were forbidden to. For some schools, the achievement record could not be verified, and for some "the verification process itself revealed a record of achievement that was not worth reporting" (115).

Schools in the study had to have test scores above the 65th percentile and 75 percent or more of their students eligible for free or reduced-price meals. In 1997, students whose families earned less than 130 percent of the poverty level ($21,385 for a family of four) were eligible for free meals, while students whose families earned less than 185 percent of the poverty level ($30,433 for a family of four) were eligible for reduced price meals.

The principals of the schools were interviewed, after which "site visits and personal interviews with the principals, teachers, students, and parents," were conducted. Most of the schools are elementary or elementary and middle, two are middle schools, and one contains grades 7 to 12.

While the vignettes provide information that is sometimes richer than what can be derived from test scores, the test scores themselves are the only common criteria of success across the schools. Unfortunately, in a number of instances, the scores come from test results provided by the school itself, not from independent sources.

One can observe that the description of how the schools were located itself contradicts the title of the report. By analogy, one could say that there are no excuses for humans not defying gravity and flying. People tried for centuries without success. Today it is commonplace because the resources necessary to fly have been put in place. That scarcely describes the condition of schools in low-income neighborhoods. It takes a great deal of power to break the bonds of gravity, and it would take a great deal of power to break the bonds of poverty on any sizable scale.

If we assume that the proportion of low-income schools is roughly the same as the proportion of students living in poverty, then there are some 17,000 low-income schools in the nation (85,000 schools, 20 percent of children in poverty). From these, the study found only twenty-one that beat the odds. And, we can note, the definition of *high poverty* in the study is more generous than the official definition of *poverty*. In the study, *high poverty* is defined as having 75 percent of students eligible for free or reduced-price meals.

If we assume for the moment that the test scores reported are real and that they reflect achievement that generalizes beyond the scores themselves (a tenuous assumption in the absence of supporting data), there are numerous variables not mentioned in the "common traits" section of the report that are more likely than those traits to contribute to success. Discussion of these variables follows.

Effort

Over and over in the report, one reads of extraordinary individuals who make extraordinary efforts. Indeed, David Levin, principal of the KIPP[2] Academy in the Bronx and Michael Feinberg of the KIPP academy in Houston state that "to replicate KIPP on a national scale, they would require a pool of educators that does not exist today. . . . In two communities that have nothing in common but a group of children abandoned by the establishment, we have opened schools that work.[3] But what we do isn't easy. First we need to find a way to make this level of commitment the standard. Then we need to make it attractive, livable, and affordable for teachers."[4] In other words, Levin is saying that it would not be reasonable to expect large numbers of teachers to make the kind of sacrifices that Levin, Feinberg, and their small cadres of teachers make.

> *Levin is saying that it would not be reasonable to expect large numbers of teachers to make the kind of sacrifices that Levin, Feinberg, and their small cadres of teachers make.*

Again, at the Wesley School in Houston, one notes another instance of the "Great Man" effect, this time of Thaddeus Lott, principal there for many years. As Gail Chaddock wrote in the *Christian Science Monitor,* "Early critics said that replicating Wesley would be tough, because you can't clone Thaddeus Lott, the large-than-life former principal who came to Wesley in 1975, or the meticulous school culture he created."[5]

Even that culture comes with heavy costs: "Turnover is high," Chaddock wrote. "There are 20 new teachers this year, out of 49. Some leave because the paperwork is crushing; others bristle at the philosophy, which allows little scope to break away from the text. Those who stay are fiercely loyal." (Note: the paperwork is not created by the Houston bureaucracy but by the record keeping of Direct Instruction and other programs in the school).

Gregory Hodge, principal of the Frederick Douglass Academy states bluntly, "Teachers don't come to the Frederick Douglass Academy to retire. They come here to make a contribution. So I ask them: Will they make the time, will they sacrifice their other commitments, do they have the skills . . . ? We spend approximately seven months a year trying to recruit teachers. I'll interview 100 to 150 teachers before I make a decision to hire" (20). If one assumes twenty-two working days in a month and 150 interviews, Hodge's schedule works out to almost one interview per day just to find one teacher. Sorta improbable.

> If one assumes twenty-two working days a month and 150 interviews, Hodge's schedule works out to almost one interview per day just to find one teacher.

At the KIPP School in Houston, "students, parents, and teachers all sign a commitment 'to do whatever it takes to learn.'" Teachers carry cellphones with toll-free numbers and are on call twenty-four hours a day to answer any concerns their students might have. "'Ten calls a night might sound like a drag,' says Feinberg, 'but everyone goes to bed ready for school the next day'" (95). One must wonder, though, how many people there are who will permit such pervasive intrusions into their private lives.

Money

Conservatives love to shout, "Don't throw money at the schools," and to claim that money does not produce increased achievement. Frankly, I have never encountered anyone who claimed that money alone would make the difference. Most people acknowledge that it is how the money is used that makes the difference, but that money must be there to be used. Money alone did not put a man on the moon, but we would never have made it to that little globe without lots of money. Conservatives, though, argue that market-oriented reforms that increase competition among schools will raise achievement with no additional expense.

The study not only does not report expenditures in a systematic way, it is seldom clear on funding sources, but clearly for some schools, even the public ones, other sources of funds are available. For the private schools, of course, there are no public funds. Marcus Garvey charges $492 a month for its elementary grades and $508 a month for high school. California's per-pupil expenditures in 1997–1998 were $5,586 (Report Card on American Education, 50).[6] The report contends that most parents cannot pay for a complete education at Garvey and that many come "for a year or two to get a foundation that their local schools have failed to provide." The brevity of the students' stay at the school makes their test scores—80th percentile in reading, 82nd in math, seem all the more remarkable. Overly so.

The report states that George Washington elementary has "supplemental money" of $350,000, "used entirely for improved instruction." It doesn't identify the source or how the school actually uses the funds.

As mentioned, the Marva Collins academy charges $4,500 tuition (this is not in the report). A Collins employee estimated that 15 percent to 25 percent of the students receive some assistance in meeting the tuition. One wonders how the 70 percent low-income families who send their children to the school meet this requirement. The Nobel system of private schools builds its schools in relatively affluent upwardly mobile neighborhoods and charges $6,000.[7]

A September 1998 press release on www.autochannel.com, announced that Cornerstone Schools received a $100,000 donation from Johnson Controls. The release read, in part, "We are pleased to join Chrysler, Ford, General Motors and many other corporate sponsors in this worthwhile effort. . . ." Said the report, "Financial gifts go a long way toward funding the school's mission, where the actual costs of an eleven-month Cornerstone education is $5,800. Parents also pay an average of $1,200.00 a year tuition."

Of the 210 students at the Fourteenth Avenue School in Newark, 76 are special education students. The report provides no information on how much money comes along with these students.

The New York branch of KIPP receives money from the New York Board of Education, but only for faculty salaries. Everything else has to be raised independently. KIPP has a well-regarded string orchestra. It has raised $70,000 for instruments.

The Healthy Start charter school in Durham, North Carolina, receives $5,300 per child from state and local sources. This compares with per-pupil expenditures of $5,541 in the nation and $4,848 in North Carolina, both figures from the 1997–1998 school year. There might be some other sources as well—starting salaries are $31,000 with a bachelor's degree and $35,000 with a master's degree. Public schools in the region begin at $22,000. In addition, the school contributes 8 percent of the salary to an IRA and awards "merit-based" bonuses from $1,000 to $2,000 per teacher.

Time

Many of the schools provide and require more time to study the material that shows up on tests than what is found in regular public schools. Earhart Elementary in Chicago, for instance, canceled all physical education, music, art, and library programs. It devotes ninety minutes each morning to reading.

Most schools offer afterschool and/or weekend programs and an extended school year. For instance, the report claims that teachers at Morse school in Cambridge, Massachusetts, are in the building from 7:30 A.M. to 5 P.M. If one adds the time needed for breakfast, dressing, and getting to the school, one wonders what kind of life the teachers have apart from the school. Cornerstone Schools, private schools in Detroit, have an eleven-month year. Healthy Start in Durham has an eleven-month year and only two weeks off at Christmas. Newberry School in Detroit maintains a four-day, two-hour after-school program in reading and math. Frederick Douglass Academy in New York is open from 7:30 A.M. to 8:00 P.M. on weekdays and 9:00 A.M. to 4:00 P.M. on Saturdays.

One of the best qualities of some of the schools also has to do with time: The schools are future-oriented. Many poor students do not develop a sense of a future. Without a sense of future, children can see little point in working hard for future rewards. Children at KIPP Academy in New York, a middle school, wear shirts that show the year they will graduate from high school. If you ask fifth graders what year they are going to college, they can tell you (although one can wonder if the children actually grasp this time span in a meaningful sense or grasp it in the way that an adult might). One principal is quoted as saying, "We talk a lot about the future, about good role models, and about careers."

Size

The report says little about class size, except in a couple of larger schools, where it is said to be above average. Conservative school critics do not favor small classes. They claim they are expensive and are largely an ineffectual way to raise achievement. They claim that "teacher quality" is more important. This is undoubtedly true in the abstract, but these critics often fail to give a precise definition of how to measure "teacher quality."

Most of the schools are small. Portland school has 152 students in PK–6, and Marcus Garvey 285 in PK-12. The largest of the schools is P. S. 161 in Brooklyn with 1,342 students in grades K–8. There is mounting evidence that small schools, as well as small classes, can improve achievement. The impact of small classes in California was small because California's approach to small classes was almost as dumb as its approach to energy deregulation. California mandated small classes without thinking about the ramifications. No one seems to have wondered where schools would find the space or the extra teachers. The mandate forced urban districts in particular to hire even more underqualified teachers.

A summary of small schools research can be found in *Small Schools, Great Strides* by Patricia Wasley, Michelle Fine, Matt Gladden, Nicole Holland, Sherry King, Esther Mosak, and Linda Powell, published in 2000 by the Bank Street College of Education, New York. A complete range of data and opinions about the impact of small classes can be found in a special issue of *Educational Evaluation and Policy Analysis*, Summer, 1999.

Selectivity

While virtually all public schools accept whomever walks in the door (magnet schools and some charters are exceptions), the schools in No Excuses select students in several ways. Some have high tuition. Some are private schools that who admit whomever they please. Two of the schools are charters. While charters in some states must admit students by lottery if they are oversubscribed, there is often selectivity in who applies and who gets in. Most charter schools do not offer transportation, making them available only to families with vehicles and flexible schedules. Some charters select by advising families that perhaps this charter school does not meet their needs (which, in some cases, could also be true). Other schools in the report have contracts with parents outlining the school's mission, setting a demand for high achievement, explaining the schools expectations for parent involvement, and detailing academic and conduct standards and penalties for noncompliance. Parents who accede to such contracts might well differ systematically from parents who do not.

Earhart elementary in Chicago is a magnet school, and magnet schools in Chicago can select students. (The term *magnet school* is not used in the report. I know this from other sources.) Not all students would be interested in the Afrocentric curriculum that Earhart says it provides. Although not stated explicitly, Douglass Academy in New York is selecting. Its seventh graders' test scores gave it a rank of 12th out of 235 middle schools in New York City. But those seventh graders would have been in the school only about six months, hardly enough time to jack the scores up that high if they were typical kids from the neighborhood. The report states that 20 percent of Douglass's students are admitted on the basis of an interview and two written recommendations.

Missing Data

The previous sections have described problems with the data that are in "No Excuses." Equally important, though, are the data that the report fails to include:

1. *Longitudinal Data.* Most of the schools do not extend beyond grade 6. In this type of study, the schools are always overwhelmingly elementary schools. This is true of the schools in the Education Trust study, as well as in the Heritage report. One likely reason for this is that standardized tests given in the elementary grades are more manipulable by extended and extensive drill-and-practice exercises.

One looks in vain for information on what happens to students in these "successful" schools once they leave them. Do they continue to score well?

The *Christian Science Monitor* reported in 1999 that Thaddeus Lott, who, as mentioned, gained considerable publicity as principal of Wesley Elementary School in Houston, is having difficulty replicating his success at the middle school to which he was later assigned. And, while the Texas Education Agency (TEA) still rates Wesley high, in 2000–2001 and 2001–2002, the school had a lower pass rate on all three of the tests that compose the Texas

> *One looks in vain for information on what happens to students in these "successful" schools once they leave them.*

Assessment of Academic Skills (TAAS) than either Houston Independent School District or the state as a whole. (The TAAS has since replaced by the purportedly harder Texas Assessment of Knowledge and Skills; data for Texas schools are available at www.tea.state.tx.us/perfreport/src/2002/campus.srch.html. Click on search by School Name and type in Wesley). The middle school, M. C. Williams, is still rated by the TEA as "low performing." According to *Monitor* reporter Gail Chaddock, Lott claims he has low middle school scores because most of the kids coming there do not come from Wesley.[8]

2. Specification of Test Data. Although the tests involved are mostly the Iowa Tests of Basic Skills, the report does not provide the norming dates. At the time of the report, Chicago was still using the 1988 norms. Repeated use of a test over a long period of time itself leads to inflated test scores.

3. Specification of Poverty Data. It is not clear where the report's poverty figures come from. Moreover, not all high-poverty neighborhoods are alike. Those composed of single family houses are likely to have far less crime, drugs, and violence than those composed of high-rise housing projects.

4. Specification of Funding. Some of the schools receive substantial funds from private sources. The report makes no systematic attempt to specify how much money the schools receive or where it comes from.

5. Specification of Staff Qualifications. The report offers no information on staff educational attainments or experience. The report mentions that the Healthy Start school in Durham deliberately does not hire certified teachers. Other than a few anecdotal reports of teacher characteristics, it provides no information about teacher qualifications.

Conclusion

The "No Excuses" report provides little information that teachers or administrators might find useful in improving the education of children living in poverty, other than to work hard for long hours. It has located some apparently exceptional principals who have hired apparently exceptional teachers and who work them very hard. These might indeed be the kind of people needed in these schools, but there is little reason to expect them to show up in great numbers.

"No Excuses" begins by stating that it is not formal research and then acting precisely as if it is. Even accepting the disclaimer at the beginning, one wonders why the study was published. No university would likely accept it as a dissertation, and no peer-reviewed journal would likely accept it for publication.

The question is, then, why did the Heritage Foundation choose to publish and publicize such a flawed report? (Some estimates contend that the Heritage Foundation often spends ten times as much to get the word out about a report as it does on the report itself.)

Possibly, Heritage had committed to put the work in play and is now stuck with that commitment. Equally plausible, however, is that the Foundation uncritically embraced the report because it supported Heritage's ideological position. It is quite possible that the Foundation has decided that rather than rely on traditional forms of propaganda, it is better to hide flawed data under the mantle of "research."

The report offers no real solution or means to a solution for the thousands of schools that it purportedly wishes to assist. In the Foreword, Adam Meyerson, Vice President for Educational Affairs for the Heritage Foundation, states baldly, "Most principals of high-poverty schools do not come close to the standard set by the No Excuses principals. They should be replaced." Given that Heritage's national search could locate only twenty-one such principals, the question to Meyerson would have to be, "By whom?"

Notes

1. This position is not the exclusive province of conservatives. The Education Trust is usually described as a liberal organization. In 2002 it published "Dispelling the Myth," in which it claimed to find thousands of "high-flying" schools characterized by high-poverty, high-minority enrollment or both. On close examination, though, the report actually proves how powerful poverty is. My debunking of this report appeared in "The Twelfth Bracey Report on the Condition of Public Education," in the October 2002 *Phi Delta Kappan.*

2. Knowledge Is Power Program.

3. New York City and Houston.

4. Since this analysis was first written, the KIPP program has received millions of dollars in underwriting from the D2F2 Foundation started by Donald and Doris Fischer, who also founded the Gap. D2F2 is quite active in promoting alternative schools having given $25 million to the California operation of Chris Whittle's Edison Schools, Inc. Whittle and other officers of Edison have repeated claimed that they will work their miracles with the same amount of money as regular public schools, but, in all instances, they have failed to do so. Without the D2F2 money, Whittle could not operate in California. For details, see "Edison's Light Dims: The Rise and Fall and Rise and Fall of H. Christopher Whittle" in this volume.

5. Gail Chaddock, "No Excuses Is the Motto at This Urban Texas Star." *Christian Science Monitor,* April 6, 1999.

6. *Report Card on American Education,* Washington, DC: American Legislative Exchange Council (annual report, authors vary).

7. This figure is now $8,500 to $10,000, depending on grade level.

8. Personal communication, February 2003.

15 The Capriciousness of High-Stakes Testing

I n June 2002, the *New York Times* reported that New York
  Regents Exams altered literature passages on its tests according
  to "sensitivity guidelines."[1] Some of the changes were ludicrous, some merely stupid, and some would lead test takers to the
wrong answer. The state promised it would never do it again, but
as the *Times'* Michael Winerip found, the censorship and bowd-
lerization is still going on. How the Department got caught and
other aspects of the affair were detailed in "The Twelfth Bracey
Report on the Condition of Public Education," published in the
Phi Delta Kappan, October 2002. More important for this essay is
a sentence in Winerip's article that draws attention to another
problem with tests—passing or failing can turn on a single item.

A statement buried in the fifteenth paragraph of Michael
Winerip's "How New York Exams Rewrite Literature (A Sequel)"[2]
deserves to be brought center stage. Winerip wrote. "In the world
of make-or-break exams, one question scored incorrectly can make
all the difference in a student's future." To people unfamiliar with
the technology of testing, Winerip's words probably look like
hyperbole. They are not. We who have worked in the field of testing have known this for some time, but the capriciousness of high-
stakes testing was revealed to the public only because of Martin
Swaden, a Minnesota parent.

Minnesota requires students to pass a test in order to obtain a high school diploma. Swaden's daughter failed. Swaden reasoned that the best way to help her next time around was to look at the test and his daughter's answer sheet to see what kinds of questions were giving her trouble. The state denied his repeated requests to see them, yielding only when he threatened to sue. (He's a lawyer, giving the threat some credibility.)

Matching his daughter's answer sheet against the key containing the officially right answers, Swaden discovered that the testing company, NCS Pearson, mis-scored six questions, enough to put his daughter over the top. She was hardly alone: 47,000 students got lower scores than they deserved, 8,000 students failed when they should have passed, and 525 seniors who had actually passed were denied the right to walk across the stage and pick up their diplomas at graduation ceremonies.

These 8,000 falsely failed students did not suffer mere temporary humiliation. Some gave up jobs to attend summer school they didn't need. Others forked out for tutors. They suffered slights from classmates. Some changed plans for the future, and some dropped out of school. They also filed a class-action suit against NCS.

> *These 8,000 falsely failed students did not suffer mere temporary humiliation. Some gave up jobs to attend summer school they didn't need.*

NCS claimed that the error was a one-time affair and couldn't happen again. It found a scapegoat and fired him. It hired the current or former state directors of testing from Virginia, Washington, and Texas to testify on its behalf. (Parents, do not expect state officials to take the lead in ferreting out errors.) The testing director from Virginia said that such errors as NCS made were likely.

The judge, though, rejected NCS's one-time-mistake arguments, concluding that NCS had a long history of shoddy quality control and had failed to hire enough employees to cure the problem. He permitted the plaintiffs to sue for punitive damages. NCS settled out of court. Some students received as much as $16,000, but most got less than $2,000. The total award amounted to over $8 million.

Test companies fail the quality control test far too often. CTB–McGraw-Hill errors forced thousands of New York City stu-

Test companies fail the quality control test far too often.

dents to attend summer school when they didn't need to. Nevada officials caught a similar error in 2002. Also in 2002, Georgia jettisoned the entire state's results on Harcourt's SAT-9—the company mis-scored all 340,000 tests. CTB–McGraw-Hill's sloppiness so offended Arizona that the state sought another contractor, but given the limited number of testing companies with the capacity to handle large state contracts, had to accept another with similar risks for errors. Basically there are only four companies: Harcourt Educational Measurement, CTB-McGraw Hill, NCS, and Riverside. Educational Testing Service, once a major player in the K–12 testing arena, has decided to become one again.

All of these errors were made before the Elementary and Secondary Education Act of 2001, the so-called No Child Left Behind Act, had any impact. That law, requiring all children in grades 3 through 8 be tested every year in reading and math (with science to be added two years later), will vastly increase the amount of testing in this country. (Some think this is no accident because the Bushes and the McGraws, who founded CTB–McGraw-Hill, have been vacation-together families for seventy-five years.) The same, short-staffed, error-prone contractors will develop and score these tests.

We can thus safely predict that test companies will make many more errors. We cannot be confident that anyone will detect and report them. Some kids will falsely flunk and some institutions will falsely bear the label—and the consequences—of being a "failing school." The states and the testing companies, fearing to look bad more than fearing to do wrong by children, will have no incentive to look for the mistakes.

We can safely predict that the test companies will make many more errors.

Indeed, one wonders how many other errors *already* lie undetected in computer files because parents from other states have not pressed to see how the tests match their children's answer sheets. They should press. No one else will. Swaden won without litigation in Minnesota. A Florida parent had to sue to see her daughter's answers and Florida governor Jeb Bush fought the suit, claiming that letting parents see their children's answer sheets would cost the state too much money. He lost.

Most parents likely don't realize how narrow and arbitrary is the difference between pass and fail. When Virginia changed its test-equating procedure for one test, the new procedure required one less item correct to pass than did the old procedure (a peculiar outcome for which the state has not accounted). That one-item difference changed 5,625 flunks into passes. (The children were informed months later that they were no longer failures.) Virginia also lowered the passing score on several of its tests in 2002, but did not apply the new standards retroactively. As a consequence, some 50,000 kids who flunked in 2000 and 2001 would have passed had they been lucky enough to take the test in 2002.

The testing industry is perhaps the largest unregulated business in the nation. There is no FDA of testing to stamp the tests for quality or make sure that the tests won't poison anyone. Legislators, governors, and boards demand accountability from teachers and school administrators, even though teachers only have control over their "products" for a few hours a day, half the year. Test companies have total control over their products. One wonders when they will be held accountable. Minnesota and Florida have made starts, but only after determined parents forced the issue. Parents in all other states should take heed.

Postscript

In March 2003, the National Bureau on Educational Testing and Public Policy at Boston College published a comprehensive review of mistakes on tests and their consequences, *Errors in Standardized Tests: A System Problem*. The monograph can be obtained at www.bc.edu/nbettp.

Notes

1. N. R. Kleinfeld, "The Elderly Man and the Sea?" *New York Times*, June 2, 2002, p. A1.

2. *New York Times*, January 8, 2003.

16 Those Misleading SAT and NAEP Trends
Simpson's Paradox at Work

The average SAT verbal score in 2002 was precisely the same as it was in 1981—504.[1] Yet, each of the six major ethnic categories used by the College Board shows an increase in that period of time: whites, 8 points; blacks, 19; Asians, 27; Puerto Ricans, 18; and American Indians, 8. How can it be, then, that all groups that make up the national average have gained, but the national average score has not budged in twenty-one years? This is not a trivial question: Critics of schools have used these national averages as indicators of no progress in education reform.

> *How can it be that all groups that make up the national average have gained, but the national average score has not budged in twenty-one years?*

The phenomenon by which the whole group shows one trend but the various subgroups show another occurs often in social science and medical research. It is known as Simpson's Paradox. A Google search on "Simpson's Paradox" produces 2,800 hits.

To understand it, let's look first at the trends for the SAT, both verbal and mathematics for the various ethnic groups and for all groups lumped together.

	Verbal			Mathematics		
	1981*	2002	Gain	1981	2002	Gain
White	519	527	+8	509	533	+24
Black	412	431	+19	391	427	+36
Asian	474	501	+27	512	569	+57
Mexican	438	446	+8	447	457	+10
Puerto Rican	437	455	+18	428	451	+23
Native American	471	479	+8	463	483	+20
All Test Takers	504	504	0	494	516	+22

*The year 1981 is used as a starting point because it was the first year the Board published a document showing SAT data by gender and ethnicity. Coincidentally, 1981 also marked the lowest point of the decline of average SAT scores that had begun in 1963. The Board category *Latin American,* which covers Central and South American students, was not in use in 1981 and currently accounts for 4 percent of all SAT test takers. They scored 458 on the verbal in 2002 and 464 on the math. Another 4 percent now check "other," also not used in 1981 and also accounts for 4 percent of the total. They scored 502 on the verbal and 514 on the math.

What on earth is going on here? The increase in math scores for the most ethnic groups exceeds, and sometimes far exceeds, the gain for all students. The verbal scores show an even more paradoxical outcome: All groups show an increase, but the gain for the whole group is exactly zero. Nil.

To understand how Simpson's Paradox affects SAT averages over time, we must look at changes in the ethnic composition of the SAT test-taking group over time. The following table shows these changes.

	1981		2002	
	#	%	#	%
White	719,383	85	698,659	65
Black	75,434	9	122,684	11
Asian	29,753	3	103,242	10
Mexican	14,405	2	48,255	4
Puerto Rican	7,038	1	14,273	1
Native American	4,655	0	7,506	1
Total		100		92

(Note: 2002 percentages do not sum to 100 percent because of 8 percent responding "Latin American" or "Other" response categories not used in 1981.)

The changing composition of the SAT test takers causes the paradox. Minorities now compose a much larger proportion of the total than they did twenty years ago. And, except for the mathematics scores of Asians, all minority scores, while rising, remain below the overall average. Adding more and more of these improving but still low scores attenuates the rise of the overall average. In the case of the verbal score, it attenuates it to zero.

Simpson's Paradox is stated in many ways. They all convey the idea that when subgroups' scores on a variable are aggregated to form a single total group, the total might show a relationship that is the reverse of the relationship seen in the subgroups. Hence, the paradox.

In the preceding example, Simpson's Paradox strikes because the composition of the whole group changes over time: many more minorities in 2002 than in 1981. Simpson's Paradox also affects one-time measurements in which the subgroups differ in some important way from the whole group. The following medical example shows how this happens. If we compare survival rates for patients in two hospitals, overall the results look like this:

	Survived	Died	Total	Survival Rate
Hospital A	800	200	1,000	80 percent
Hospital B	900	100	1,000	90 percent

Hospitals are dangerous places generally, but it looks like if you must check into one, Hospital B is your medical facility of choice. But what if we divide the patients into those who were in good condition prior to treatment and those who were in poor condition?

	Survived	Died	Total	Survival Rate
Good-Condition Patients				
Hospital A	590	10	600	98 percent
Hospital B	870	30	900	97 percent
Poor-Condition Patients				
Hospital A	210	190	400	53 percent
Hospital B	30	70	100	30 percent

Thus, while Hospital B had a higher survival rate for all patients than did Hospital A, Hospital A treated a higher proportion of those who were in bad shape to start with. It also managed to keep a higher proportion of that group alive. Hospital A is the place for you whether you are in good or poor condition on your arrival.

Back in education, we see Simpson's Paradox at work in NAEP trends, as well as in SAT trends.

NAEP Reading	1971	1999
Age 17	285	288
Age 13	255	259
Age 9	208	212

Over a period of twenty-eight years, scores change little. "NAEP reading scores are essentially unchanged," said Right-wing pundit, George F. Will in his March 2, 2003 column for the *Washington Post*. "This refutes the durable delusion that schools' cognitive outputs vary directly with financial inputs." This is a common comment from the Right. Spending has increased (*soared, skyrocketed, mounted* are words commonly used by the critics), but test scores are *flat* (*stagnant, sluggish, static,* choose your term). As with the SAT, though, looking at trends by ethnic group reveals something different than just looking at aggregates for all groups:

Reading	White		Black		Hispanic	
	1971	1999	1971	1999	1975*	1999
Age 17	291	295	238	264	252	271
Age 13	261	267	222	238	232	244
Age 9	212	221	170	186	183	193

*Hispanics constituted too small a sample to generate a reliable estimate in the 1971 assessment. Asians were still too small a group in 1999.

The changes for white students pretty much mirror the changes for the whole sample. The gains for black and Hispanic students, though, are much larger than for the entire group. However, their scores remain lower than those of whites and, by Simpson's Paradox, because they are now a larger proportion of the total group, they attenuate the gains seen when all groups are combined.

The proportion of whites in the sample falls from roughly 80 percent to roughly 70 percent (varying slightly for different ages). The proportion of the entire group made up of blacks changes over time from about 14 percent to about 16 percent, while the proportion of Hispanics doubles from about 5 percent to about 10 percent). Asians were not represented as a separate group until the science assessment of 1996, and even in that year there was concern about the accuracy of the estimated scores. NAEP assessments in mathematics and science also show larger gains for ethnic groups than for everyone taken as a whole.

Lest anyone still be mystified by what's going on, let me present a hypothetical but concrete example. Consider the following scores:

	Time 1	Time 2
1.	500	510
2.	500	510
3	500	510
4.	500	510
5.	500	510
6.	500	510
7.	500	510
8.	500	430
9.	500	430
10.	400	430
Avg.	490	486

Let's assume that all of those 500s at Time 1 represent the SAT scores of white kids and that the 400 represents the SAT scores of minority students. At Time 2, assume that the 510s are the SAT scores of white students, and the 430s the SATs of minorities. So, all groups have gained. Whites have gained 10 points, and minorities 30 points. The difference is that at Time 1, minorities only made up 10 percent of the total group, but that at Time 2, they constitute 30 percent of the total. When we calculate the average for Time 1 and Time 2, we find that, despite the fact that all groups are scoring higher at Time 2, the

> Critics have ignored Simpson's Paradox not only conveniently, but also deliberately. And unethically.

average at Time 2 is lower than at Time 1: 486 at Time 2 versus 490 at Time 1. This is Simpson's Paradox.

Thus, it sometimes appears as if test scores are not rising, or are even falling when, in fact, test scores for all groups are rising at the same time as lower scoring groups are making up a larger proportion of the total. This, it should be obvious, does not mean the same thing as falling test scores due to declining achievement. It *should* be obvious, but it is often conveniently overlooked by school critics. Indeed, because these critics are statistically sophisticated, one must conclude that they have ignored Simpson's Paradox not only conveniently, but also deliberately. And unethically.

Note

1. The College Board "recentered" the SAT in 1995. The 504 is the score for both years obtained using the recentered SAT. Using the original scale for both years would yield the same result although the number would not be 504.

17   The Dumbing of America?

A slightly abbreviated version of this essay appeared in the November 1997 issue of *American Heritage*. It provides a brief history of criticism of American schools. A more complete history can be found in *Final Exam: A Study of the Perpetual Scrutiny of American Schools*, published in 1995 by the Agency for Instructional Technology in Bloomington, Indiana.

I first noticed the nostalgia for some (nonexistent) Golden Age of American Education while researching my first article about education criticism and education reform. To try and dispel this nostalgia, I titled my piece "Why Can't They Be Like We Were?" a snippet of a lyric from the 1960 musical "Bye Bye Birdie." The lyric continues, "perfect in every way? Oh, what's the matter with kids today."

> *The nostalgics forget that a century ago, the high school graduation rate was about 3 percent.*

At one point in *The Thirteenth Man*, former Secretary of Education Terrel Bell reflects on his perception of educational decline (1): "If we are frank with ourselves, we must acknowledge that for most Americans . . . neither diligence in learning nor rigorous standards of performance prevail. . . . How do we once again become a nation of learners, in which attitudes towards intellectual pursuit and quality of work have excellence at their core?" (167)

Terrel Bell displays two common qualities of educational reformers since World War II: nostalgia and amnesia.

In penning these words, Bell displayed two common qualities of educational reformers since World War II: nostalgia and amnesia. They look back through a haze to some imagined Golden Era of American education when we were, in Bell's words, "a nation of learners." The nostalgics forget that the inscription on the base of the Statue of Liberty does not read "Send me your college grads, your 1200 SATs yearning to learn." They forget that a century ago, the high school graduation rate was about 3 percent. They forget that that graduation rate did not exceed 50 percent until after World War II. (The current on-time graduation rate is 83 percent. If one adds in those who receive a GED or who drop out but then return for a diploma, the rate rises to 91 percent.) They forget that until recently it was assumed that no more than 20 percent of American youth could handle a college curriculum; now, almost two-thirds of all high school graduates are enrolled in college the following fall.

Yet our schools have been assailed decade after decade—in the 1950s they were assailed for failing to do enough in the space and weapons races; in the 1960s for not bringing about integration fast enough; in the 1970s for not being warm and cuddly enough; in the 1980s for letting the country down in its race to compete in the global marketplace.

In addition to these unrealistic expectations, since 1980, public education has been victimized by those who, while holding the highest office in the public school system, deliberately attempted, and continue to attempt, to destroy the system. Foremost among these are former Secretaries of Education, William Bennett and Lamar Alexander.

Ronald Reagan entered the presidency with an educational agenda of school prayer, tuition tax cuts, and vouchers. George H. W. Bush pushed even more energetically for privatization of schools. During the twelve years of these administrations, reports containing positive comments and findings about American schools were deliberately suppressed. The assault continued. On

July 18, 1996, presidential candidate, Robert Dole, spoke on education, once again calling for vouchers to privatize the system. According to reports on National Public Radio's "All Things Considered," the speech was written by Bennett and Alexander, who "sat nearby, smiling as it was delivered."

But people like Bennett and Alexander, driven with a strange mixture of ideology, expedience, and belief in a free market approach to schools, were hardly alone. Many educators have also been critical of public schools and attacked their performance with an intensity unlike that found directed at any other institution in public affairs. Consider these three comments:

> The achievement of U. S. students in grades K–12 is very poor.
>
> American students are performing at much lower levels than students in other industrialized nations.
>
> International examinations designed to compare students from all over the world usually show American students at or near the bottom.

These are powerful indictments. As we shall see, none of them is true, but their source is as remarkable as their content. These are the opening sentences from three consecutive 1993 weekly columns in the *New York Times* by Albert Shanker, then president of the American Federation of Teachers. One would think that, if only to mollify the 800,000 members of his union, Shanker would have been a little more enthusiastic about what his teachers have accomplished.

While Shanker might have been a little more abrasive than most, many within the field of education have shown minimal support for public schools. After all, virtually all of the forty-three background papers commissioned by the National Commission on Excellence in Education, the group that produced "A Nation At Risk," were authored by professors of education.

It is impossible to imagine a Secretary of Defense lambasting the weapons industry or a Secretary of Commerce chastising American industry for its accomplishments the way Secretaries of Education have demeaned the performance of American public schools. How and why did people within the field arrive at such a view of the schools, and what does the evidence really say?

We begin the chronicle in 1893 with the Committee on Secondary Schools Studies, better known simply as the Committee of Ten after its makeup of five college presidents and five public school superintendents. The Committee of Ten can be considered the first in a long line of "blue ribbon commissions" to examine American education.

When the Committee of Ten began its work, there was little to examine, and, indeed, the principal goal of the Committee was to bring some kind of coherence to a "system" that had largely grown without organization or clarity of purpose. In 1890, we were a nation of 63 million people, but only 203,000 of them attended secondary school. Another 3 million age-eligible children were not enrolled. A nation of learners, indeed! In fact, one wonders, after reading the Committee's report, what those children who were enrolled in school did all day:

> As things are now, the high school teacher finds in the pupils fresh from the grammar schools no foundation of elementary mathematical conceptions outside of arithmetic; no acquaintance with algebraic language; and no accurate knowledge of geometrical forms. As to botany, zoology, chemistry, and physics, the minds of pupils entering the high school are ordinarily blank on these subjects. When college professors endeavor to teach chemistry, physics, botany, zoology, meteorology, or geology to persons of eighteen or twenty years of age, they discover that in most instances new habits of observing, reflecting, and recording have to be painfully acquired—habits which they should have acquired in early childhood. The college teacher of history finds in like manner that his subject has never taken any serious hold on the minds of pupils fresh from secondary schools.

Why were the children's heads so empty? A look at what went on in schools provides part of the answer. Contemporary critics often claim that life in classrooms hasn't changed in a century. The reflections of educator Ralph Tyler, however, contradict this contention. Tyler was one of the most prolific writers and innovators the field has known, working actively until his death in 1994 at age ninety-two. Among other things, Tyler directed the Institute for Advanced Study at Stanford University for a number of years and was also the principal architect of the National Assessment of Educational Progress in the 1960s. When a mere sprite of seventy-two, Tyler looked back on what schools had been like and had this to say:

> What I remember from my experience as a pupil are the strict-ness of discipline, the catechismic type of recitation, the dull-ness of the textbooks, and the complete absence of any obvi-ous connection between our classwork and the activities we carried on outside of school. . . . The view held by most teach-ers and parents was that the school was quite separate from the other institutions in society and its tasks should be sufficiently distasteful to the pupils to require strong discipline to under-take them and carry them through. Furthermore, they believed that while in school children should not talk with one another; all communication should be between the teacher and the class as a whole or between the teacher and the individual pupil.[1]

Other accounts confirm Tyler's comment on the prevalence of recitation as the principal classroom activity. Tyler's school does not strike one as an institution to inspire a generation of life-long learners. Indeed, one can wonder how *any* scholars emerged from such stultifying environments.

After the Committee of Ten's 1893 report, secondary educa-tion expanded rapidly, but remained in disarray as educators debated what the high school curriculum should look like. *The School Review*, the principal journal of secondary education at the time, was filled with titles cast as questions: "What Should the Modern Secondary School Aim to Accomplish?" "What Studies Should Predominate in Secondary School?" "What Ought the Study of Mathematics Contribute to the Education of the High School Pupil?" "What Is the Consensus of Opinion as to the Place of Science in the Preparatory Schools?" "Can American History Be Put into All Courses in the High School?" This is a partial list of titles from the 1897 volume alone.

As educators attempted to answer such questions, they ignored two aspects of education that dominate current discus-sion: the outcomes of education and the school-to-work transi-tion. Although few students graduated from high school and few of those went on to college, the secondary curriculum was ori-ented toward providing courses acceptable to the institutions of higher education. Indeed, the colleges and universities were seen, at least implicitly, as the keepers of educational standards. The

Committee of Ten, in any case, recommended a high school curriculum that we today would call college preparatory.

In addition, the field's thinking about pedagogy was dominated at the time by faculty psychology. Faculty psychology contended that the mind consisted of faculties that were quite analogous to muscles. Like muscles, faculties grew and were strengthened through exercise. The principal means of exercising the faculties were mathematics, Greek, and Latin. Natural sciences were only beginning to attain credibility as courses of study on a par with these three. No one, apparently, had thought about developing any direct measures of these faculties and their proper use in order to determine how well the schools were developing them.

There was, at this time, no concern for any vocational aspect of schools. In addition to getting students ready for college, schools retained the civic functions Jefferson had sought for them. Schools *had* been recognized as important ladders up the scale of economic well-being, but there is no indication that anyone thought that schools themselves were important to the economic well-being of the nation. (At the elementary level, schools civic function did include the Americanization of immigrants.) How could such a sparsely attended institution as the high school have much to say on this matter? The notion that schools were somehow important to the well-being of the nation would await end of World War II.

From 1910 to 1945 secondary schools expanded rapidly, the graduation rate rising from 10 percent to 45 percent. The expansion does not seem to have been accompanied by any coherence however. In 1932, the Progressive Education Association noted that secondary education

> *did not have a clear purpose . . . it did not prepare students adequately for the responsibilities of community life. . . . The high school seldom challenged the student of first-rate ability to work up to the level of his intellectual powers. . . . The conventional high school curriculum was far removed from the real concerns of youth. . . . Finally, the relation of school and college was unsatisfactory to both institutions".* [Italics are in the original]

Criticism during this period was, in the words of one observer, "always abundant," but it hadn't taken on the tone that schools had failed. Since 1912, the United States had become obsessed with efficiency. A certain Frederick Winslow Taylor had come on the scene, touting something he called "scientific management." In this, the decade of the muckrakers, Taylor's concerns with efficiency became immensely popular. In the schools, scientific management had little to do with what students were learning or how well, but with efficiencies of various sorts that would save money. The comment of the California Taxpayers Association, is typical:

> The Taxpayers Association of California exists for the purpose of eliminating waste and promoting greater efficiency in the administration of public affairs. As part of its operating program it will attempt to show the businessmen and taxpayers of California how they can get better educational results for the money spent. Educational leaders for many years have been demanding changes for the better, but either have achieved no results or else have had to be satisfied with so many compromises that it is generally admitted that the highest efficiency is not being obtained even with the large amount of money now being spent.[2]

This concern with efficiency had nothing to do with learning. If one reads the *American School Boards Journal* of these years, the principal forum for school administrators, one finds little said about learning and a great deal said about counting. In *Education and the Cult of Efficiency*, Raymond Callahan refers to this period and its activities as "The Descent into Trivia." The descent produced such books as *Economy in Education,* in which U.S. Commissioner of Education William J. Cooper noted,

> One superintendent in Kansas had reported that through cooperative buying, he was able to save over 40 percent on paper fasteners, 25 percent on thumbtacks, 20 percent on theme paper, 30 percent on colored pencils, and 50 percent on hectograph paper. In another instance, one school board had discovered that it paid 50 cents a ton more for coal than some boards. (in Callahan, 241)

Cooper then gave a series of suggestions for economizing:

> Frequently schools purchase ink by the quart, paying a good price for it and still more for its transportation. If one makes ink

from ink powder, he will usually have an article which is good
enough for schoolwork. Money could also be saved on lumber
for manual training classes by purchasing odd lengths of
ungraded lumber which could be bought for 1/3 the price of
first class material.(in Callahan, 241)

On the matter of school paper, Cooper noted,

> There is always some waste. A sheet may be larger than needed.
> The best remedy for this is to supply two sizes, one the regular
> 8 1/2" by 11", the other 8 1/2" by 5 1/2". If the superintendent
> will study his paper and its uses he will be able to eliminate odd
> sizes and buy more standard sizes. (in Callahan, 241)

The few studies that did look at academic outcomes of education found them wanting, but the authors of the reports did not
seem inclined to blame the schools. Through the history department of Columbia University, the *New York Times* studied students'
knowledge of American history and geography. The *Times* published its findings on April 4, 1943. It was appalled at the results:

> A large majority of the students showed that they had virtually
> no knowledge of elementary aspects of American history. They
> could not identify such names as Abraham Lincoln, Thomas
> Jefferson, Andrew Jackson or Theodore Roosevelt. . . . Most of
> the students do not have the faintest notion of what this coun-
> try looks like. St. Louis was placed on the Pacific Ocean, Lake
> Huron, Lake Erie, the Atlantic Ocean, Ohio River, St. Lawrence
> River, and almost everyplace else. (A1)

"Hundreds of students thought Walt Whitman was a band-
leader," huffed the Gray Lady. Because the editors made no further comment on this finding, we can conclude that they did not
make the connection to Paul Whiteman, who led a popular jazz
orchestra (a 2003 radio commentary off-handedly referred to
Whiteman as "the Elvis of his day").

The *Times* also did not comment on what surely was the most
damning aspect of its findings: The study had been conducted on
college freshmen. At the time, about 45 percent of students graduated from high school, and of these, about 15 percent went on
to college. Thus, the survey had uncovered not just a group of
ignoramuses, but an *elite* of ignoramuses.

The *Times* was incensed enough to put the story on page 1, next to its major headline of the day, "Patton Attacks East of El Guettar." It devoted several pages inside to the results of the survey, but it made no attempt to discover why students knew so little or to lay blame. It described the study as one to discover how much material learned in secondary school was retained in college. At the time, colleges argued that they did not need to teach history because it had been taught to all in high school. Finding little retention, the *Times* dismissed this argument. Apparently, the *Times* assumed that the students once knew the material and had simply forgotten it. It did not consider the possibility that the material was not taught or was taught poorly.

After World War II, though, the educational failings of students were more and more ascribed to problems in the schools. In the immediate postwar period, one finds for the first time declarations of decline and a sense that things used to be better. The criticism from World War II was so chronic and intense that in 1989, the eminent education historian Lawrence Cremin looked back in perplexity:

> The popularization of American schools and colleges since the end of World War II has been nothing short of phenomenal, involving an unprecedented broadening of access, an unprecedented diversification of curricula, and an unprecedented extension of public control. In 1950, 34 percent of the American population twenty-five years of age or older had completed at least four years of high school, while 6 percent of that population had completed at least four years of college. By 1985, 74 percent of the American population twenty-five years or older had completed at least four years of high school, while 19 percent had completed at least four years of college. During the same 35 year period, school and college curricula broadened and diversified tremendously. . . .
>
> Yet this [expansion of schooling] seemed to bring with it a pervasive sense of failure. The question would have to be "Why?"[3]

Indeed, that is the question. The answer is complex. In part, it lies in the very success of schools at providing nearly universal secondary education. At the end of the war, secondary enrollments approached 90 percent.[4] Not all were exposed to the same curriculum, however. In 1945, a conference asked how the schools should cope with their expanding clientele. At the time, many educators were strongly influenced by the recently developed field of psychometrics, or test making. Many test makers claimed that intellectual ability was inherited and that, overall, such ability was distributed in the national population in a normal curve. With these notions in mind, the conference decided that no more than 20 percent of high school students would ever go to college. Another 20 percent could be handled adequately by the recently developed vocational programs. That left 60 percent of the students with no curriculum that served their needs.

The conference decided to build a curriculum for this "forgotten 60 percent" around the "needs of students." These needs led to the development of what the conferees called Life Adjustment Education. Life Adjustment Education was a genuine attempt to adapt secondary schools to an increasingly diverse population, but it was based on the assumption that the students couldn't be challenged academically. It was an intellectually weak pedagogy and open to easy ridicule. How would the "needs of students" be determined? In many instances, through the administration of questionnaires to the students themselves. But teenagers then, as today, saw their needs in terms of how to make friends, get along with the opposite sex, and a host of other short-term "needs."

The faculties of arts and sciences in various universities already harbored suspicions about the intellectual capacity of schools of education. When these schools now started discussing Life Adjustment Education, the liberal arts faculties exploded in derision. Progressive Education with its emphasis on the present was bad enough. Life Adjustment Education was intolerable.

Foremost among the Life Adjustment critics was Arthur Bestor, a professor of history at the University of Illinois. Bestor's popular 1953 book was titled, *Educational Wastelands: The Retreat from Learning in Our Public Schools*. Note the word *retreat*. This appears to be the first time that a critique of the schools harkened back to a previous time when conditions were better.

Bestor loaded *Wastelands* with statistics to show that schools were, indeed, retreating. He observed, for instance, that "Fifty years ago, *half* of all students in public schools were studying Latin; today less than a quarter are enrolled in courses in *all* foreign languages." This was a curious lapse in logic for a historian. Bestor failed to note that fifty years prior to his book, only 50 percent of students were enrolled in *any* school, and only 7 percent of all students graduated from high school. A quarter of the current crop of students was actually a lot more students than half of the students fifty years earlier.

Thus, part of the sense of failure stemmed from criticism of attempts to adapt the school to what were referred to as the "new learners." A more important part of the sense of failure derived from America's changed role in the world. No longer able to retreat into isolationism, the United States now confronted the Soviet Union for ideological and technological domination of the globe, seeking to win the space and weapons races without destroying the globe in the process. Wrote the Committee on the Clear and Present Danger, "We need not only trained men but also the most modern weapons. . . . This means we need both a reservoir of trained men and a continuing advance on every scientific and technical front." "It is men that count," said James B. Conant, former President of Harvard and critic of American high schools.

The most vocal commentator on the need for manpower was Admiral Hyman G. Rickover, widely credited with the development of America's nuclear navy. "Let us never forget," said Rickover," that there can be no second place in a contest with Russia and that there will be no second chance if we lose."[5] Armed with statistics from Allen Dulles, head of the CIA, Rickover stumped the country and harangued congressmen on the need for more scientists, engineers, and mathematicians. The Russians, Dulles's statistics allegedly showed, were outstripping us in these vital areas.

Where would we get the manpower we needed? Well, where else, but the schools? For the first time in the nation's history, people looked at schools as integral to national security. And schools weren't carrying their weight.

Into this tense, insecure atmosphere, the Russians launched *Sputnik*, the first man-made satellite to circle the globe. To the school critics, this small sphere offered proof that they had been right. The schools were failing. *Sputnik* was flung into orbit in October 1957. By March 1958, *Life* magazine, among others, had readied a long, four-part series on "The Crisis in Education." The cover of the March 24, 1958, edition showed a stern-looking Alexei

When Sputnik *was launched in 1957, school critics thought it was proof that schools were failing.*

Kutzkov staring out from Moscow, while Stephen Lapekas gazed out from Chicago with an easy smile. Inside, pictures showed Kutzkov conducting complex experiments in physics and chemistry and even reading *Sister Carrie* out loud in English class. Lapekas was shown walking hand-in-hand with his girlfriend, rehearsing a musical and in other activities that stressed the social and downplayed the academic, a life without rigor. In the one picture that dealt with Lapekas's academic life, he is shown retreating from a geometry problem on the blackboard, laughing, as are his classmates. The caption explains, "Stephen amused the class with wisecracks about his ineptitude."

Life brought in Sloan Wilson, author of *The Man in the Gray Flannel Suit,* for a two-page essay, "It's Time to Close Our Circus." As with Bestor, Wilson saw failure and a decline from previous accomplishments:

> The facts of the school crisis are all out and in plain sight and pretty dreadful to look at. First of all it has been shown that a surprisingly small percentage of high school students is studying what used to be considered basic subjects . . . People are complaining that the diploma has been devalued to the point of meaninglessness. . . . It is hard to deny that America's schools, which were supposed to reflect one of history's noblest dreams and to cultivate the nation's youthful minds, have degenerated into a system for coddling and entertaining the mediocre.[6]

We imagine Wilson toying with a next sentence that would begin "The foundations of our society are threatened by a rising tide of mediocrity." That sentence had to wait twenty-five years, though, to appear in another major critique of schools—1983's, "A Nation At Risk." Still, Wilson had found a similar current almost precisely twenty-five years earlier. At the time, there were precious few *data* about school performance, but what there were contradicted Wilson and other critics. Although the number of people taking the SAT had increased from 10,654 in 1941 to 376,800 in 1957, the scores remained at the 1941 levels.[7] The SATs were at the level established in the standard-setting year of 1941. Scores on achievement tests had been steadily rising.

Although "A Nation At Risk" was the next great critique, the period from 1957 to 1983 was scarcely without criticism of the schools. American schools have often been faulted for not solving social problems, and in the Sixties, they were harshly criticized for failing to achieve racial integration soon enough. While schools were taking the blame for continued segregation, the verdict arrived on the grand curriculum reforms that followed *Sputnik:* They had failed.

Reformers held out great hopes for the New Math and its attendant innovation in other fields. Prominent professors had given up their research and publishing careers to develop these curricula. That the new curricula were being developed by some of the finest minds at some of our finest universities was initially thought to be their greatest strength. Later, these qualities were recognized as their greatest weakness. Although eminent in their fields, the scholars had no sense of how a classroom works. They tried to create materials that "would permit scholars to speak directly to the child," without the intervention of teachers, whose abilities were suspect. The materials should be "teacher-proof." This feature alone guaranteed failure.

About the same time as the new curricula were pronounced dead, books such as *Death at an Early Age, 36 Children,* and *The Way It Spozed to Be* appeared. While most of these books described how schools were failing minority students, some, like *How Children Fail,* were general indictments of schools and led to a widespread feeling that schools were simply not good places for children to be. "Free schools" and "alternative schools" began to spring up around the country. (Some veterans of this movement have been active in the more recent trend toward charter schools.) Charles Silberman summed up the anti-school feeling in his influential 1970 *Crisis in the Classroom* (Random House).

Silberman's opus appeared when the Red Menace still hung over our heads. Domestic events had created the feeling that nothing was secure: the Free Speech Movement, the Civil Rights Movement, the Summer of Love, Vietnam, the Watts riots and the many urban uprisings that followed, the Chicago Police Riot, the Vietnam Moratorium, Kent State, Woodstock, Altamont, and the assassinations of Robert F. Kennedy, Martin Luther King, Jr., and Malcolm X. Campuses and streets were patrolled by Students for a Democratic Society and the Black Panthers. Fortress America seemed very vulnerable, indeed, to both physical and cultural barbarians.

In this milieu, Silberman asked what the fuss was all about. He observed that in a review of 186 "then and now" studies, all but 10 had favored "now." Then-and-now studies compare achievement at two points in time. The Department of Health, Education, and Welfare examined the review and concluded, "Until better evidence is presented, the tentative judgment must be that American children in the sixties are learning more than their older brothers and sisters learned in the fifties" (in Silberman, 18).

Silberman was perplexed: "Why, then, the pervasive sense of crisis? How to explain the fact that an educational system that appears to be superbly successful from one standpoint appears to be in grave trouble from another?" Silberman clearly had the social unrest of both urban blacks and suburban whites in mind when he suggested,

> The question cannot be answered with regard to education alone; it is the central paradox of American life. In almost every area, improvements beyond what anyone thought possible fifty or twenty-five or even ten years ago have produced anger and anxiety rather than satisfaction.
>
> It is only when men sense the possibility of improvement, in fact, that they become dissatisfied with their situation and rebel against it. . . . This retroactive impatience over things previously accepted in turn leads men to misconstrue improvement in their condition as deterioration. (19)

But such improvements in schools as Silberman found did not mean there was no crisis:

> The need of the moment, clearly, is not to celebrate our successes but to locate and remedy the weaknesses and failures. The test of a society, as of an institution, is not whether it is improving, although certainly such a test is relevant, but whether it is adequate to the needs of the present and of the foreseeable future. Our educating institutions fail that test: schools, colleges, churches, newspapers, magazines, television stations, and networks, all fall short of what they could be, of what they must be if we are to find meaning and purpose in our lives, in our society, and in our world. (29)

Thus, Silberman rejected the nostalgia of many critics, but found a crisis in the relationship between what schools are and what they could be. Silberman accepted that kids were learning more and concentrated more on the quality of life in schools. He found it wanting, to say the least:

> Because adults take schools so much for granted, they fail to appreciate what grim joyless places most American schools are, how oppressive and petty are the rules by which they're governed, how intellectually sterile and aesthetically barren, what an appalling lack of civility obtains on the part of teachers and principals, what contempt they consciously display for children as children.
>
> The most important characteristic schools share in common is a preoccupation with order and control. (10)

It is not clear that Silberman's characterization of schools was accurate, but it fit well with the descriptions found in some of the other books mentioned previously. To cure the ills, Silberman offered the same prescription that Joseph Featherstone had offered three years earlier in three articles in the *New Republic*: open education, a British import.[8] Open education made the classroom more informal. Originally intended only for five- to seven-year-olds, it was quickly misadapted to all ages in this country.

Silberman's statement that children today knew more than ever appeared early in the book, but was lost in the next five hundred pages describing the "crisis" and how to cure it. Whatever currency it might have had was buried seven years later when the College Board called attention to what was then a little attended fact: SAT scores had been falling for fourteen years. The Board formed a panel, headed by former Secretary of Labor Willard Wirtz, to study the decline.

The Wirtz panel attributed most of the decline to changes in who was taking the test: more women, more minorities, more students with mediocre high school records, and more students from low-income families. The co-chair of the panel, former U.S. Commissioner of Education Harold Howe II, wrote an article entitled "Let's Have Another SAT Decline." Howe contended that the civil rights agenda of education was unfinished, that the doors needed to be opened wider, and if this caused the scores to drop again, so be it and so what?

The Wirtz panel emphasized the complexity of the decline. One of its background papers simply listed the number of hypotheses brought forward to explain the fall: There were eighty-seven of them, not including one from a physicist that claimed the decline was due to the radioactive fallout from the nuclear testing programs of the Fifties (some people thought that might have been a satire).

The media and the public had a simpler interpretation: The American high school was failing. The developers of the SAT referred to it as a "mere supplement," but the public now saw it as the platinum rod for measuring school performance. That performance was plummeting. The stage was set for "A Nation At Risk."

Beginning in 1980, a new diagnosis about what was wrong with American schools appeared and a new prescription was brought forward about how to cure the crisis in American education. Policy papers written for presidential candidate Ronald Reagan concluded that the [putative] decline of American schools was largely due to a force heretofore seen as a powerful remedy: the federal government. Following arguments made by Milton Friedman in his 1962 book, *Capitalism and Freedom*, advisers to Reagan argued that the U.S. Department of Education, only recently created, should be abolished. In addition, tuition tax credits and vouchers should be provided to parents to permit them to choose where to send their kids to school. In the free market system that would follow this program, good schools would flourish and bad schools would go out of business. Previous perceptions of educational problems and/or decline had resulted in increased federal efforts. Those efforts, the new philosophy contended, were part and parcel of the problem.

Reagan appointed Terrel Bell of Utah as Secretary of Education with the, no doubt, apocryphal instructions not to unpack his suitcase once he arrived in Washington. (Reagan *had* promised to abolish the department.) In his book about life with a boss who is trying to do away with your job, Bell reported he heard constant criticisms about the state of American education and began to long for an event that, like *Sputnik*, would shake us out of our complacency. No such event was forthcoming, and Bell fell back on establishing a blue ribbon commission.

It is clear that this group, the National Commission on Educational Excellence, was not free to peruse the data and establish the actual condition of America's schools. Nor did they concern themselves with the quality-of-life issues that Silberman had

addressed. The commission was there to document all of the terrible things Bell had heard. And that is what it did. Its report, "A
Nation At Risk," is one of the most selective uses of data for propaganda purposes in the history of education. After its opening
statement about the tide of mediocrity and how, if an unfriendly
foreign power had foisted our schools on us we might have considered it an act of war, "Risk" went on to list thirteen indicators
of why we are a nation at risk. As noted, these indicators are
highly selected and presented in misleading statements.

For instance, one statement reads, "There was a steady
decline in science achievement scores of U.S. 17-year-olds as
measured by national assessments of science in 1969, 1973, and
1977." This statement, as far as it goes, is true. But a disinterested
observer would note immediately that it does not go far. Why
does it pick on seventeen-year-olds? Why does it pick on science?
The answer is: It is only the trend of science scores for seventeen-
year-olds that supports the crisis rhetoric. The science scores of
nine- and thirteen-year olds do not. The reading and math scores
of nine-, thirteen- and seventeen-year-olds in reading and mathematics were all either steady or rising. Of nine trend lines, only
one could be used to allege a crisis. That was the one the
Commission reported (for more on the selective spinning of statistics in "Risk," see Chapter 10, "April Foolishness: 'A Nation At
Risk' at Twenty").

The education community should have risen to its feet and
said of "Risk," "This is garbage." Which it was. But many educational organizations' policies are influenced by how they see an
event affecting the availability of funds. "Risk" depicted problems.
Surely that meant, as it had in the past, that money would flow in
order to fix them. Educational organizations, if not people at the
school level, enthusiastically accepted the report.

"Risk" embraced a new and powerful, if erroneous, conclusion: Schools are tightly linked to the performance of the U.S.
economy and our ability to compete in the global marketplace. In
fact, "competition in the global marketplace" soon became the
cliche of the 80s. It replaced the Red Menace as a scare phrase.
When a recession arrived in the late 1980s, this putative link
allowed people to blame the schools. The schools are not, of
course, tightly linked to the performance of economies, ours or
others.[9] Historian Cremin noted this very clearly:

American economic competitiveness with Japan and other nations is to a considerable degree a function of monetary, trade, and industrial policy, and of decisions made by the President and Congress, the Federal Reserve Board, and the federal departments of the Treasury and Commerce and Labor.

Therefore, to contend that problems of international competitiveness can be solved by educational reform, especially educational reform defined solely as school reform, is not merely Utopian and millenialist, it is at best foolish and at worst a crass effort to direct attention away from those truly responsible for doing something about competitiveness and to lay the burden on the schools. (102–103)

Crass effort or not, it worked and continues to work. Fortunately, the economy did not listen. Starting in 1994, one began to see headlines heralding the recovery: "The American Economy, Back on Top," trumpeted the Sunday business section of the *New York Times*. "America Cranks It Up," said *Business Week* at the same time. The Geneva-based World Economic Forum pronounced the U.S. economy the most competitive in the world among twenty-five developed nations in both 1994 and 1995. In 1996, the Forum changed its formula and the U.S. "fell" to fourth place. The International Institute for Management retained a formula similar to the Forum's old one, and the U.S. maintained its place as number one.

Stanford University professor Larry Cuban, noting that the schools were blamed for the recession of the late Eighties and given no credit for the recovery of the Nineties, observed like Cremin before him that the link was not there. To use the title of Cuban's article on the topic, the link between schools and the economy is "The Great School Scam."[10]

Yet, people continue to link schools and the economy in ways unflattering to the schools. "The system is broken," said IBM CEO Louis V. Gerstner, referring to the schools at the "summit" he organized with the nation's governors in March, 1996. Because the summit emphasized technology, some saw Gerstner's comments as self-serving, coming from a man with computers to sell.[11]

In the debate over schools and their relationship to the economy, there has been a not so subtle shift in talk about the purpose of schooling. The civic functions of schooling have been lost. There is some talk about the importance of schooling to personal advancement. There is little talk about education as the means to producing well-rounded people. But most discussions about schooling have been cast in the dreary instrumentality of getting a job, or, to use the cliche of the moment, the "school-to-work" transition. The talk is of what business needs—demands!—of schools and how schools should supply it.

Of course, there has never been anything approaching unanimity on the purpose of education in this nation or elsewhere. Aristotle, after all, observed that education dealt with "the good life" and that people would always disagree on what the good life consisted of. To see it solely in terms of getting and keeping a job, though, is rather new to this country.

Our preeminent educational influence, Thomas Jefferson, saw education as having two purposes. On the one hand, it would act as a great sorting machine that would ensure that "the best geniuses would be annually raked from the rubbish," creating an "aristocracy of worth and genius" as opposed to an aristocracy of blood, which so afflicted Europe. On the other hand, to protect the nation from the "germ of corruption" that Jefferson saw as infecting all governments, the power had to ultimately reside in the people, and to protect even them, "their minds must be improved to a certain degree" through schooling for all.[12]

Even Jefferson's more practical peer, Benjamin Franklin, did not argue for vocational training in school. Noting that people in a developing nation would need many skills, Franklin saw his own Philadelphia school as a place where young men "will come out . . . fitted for learning any business calling or profession." Franklin sounds eerily like former Secretary of Labor Robert Reich contending that the most valuable skill that might be learned in school today is "flexibility." In any case, specific vocational concerns began to creep into educational discussion early in this century as secondary schooling began its rapid expansion.

Some of the possible purposes of education are in direct conflict, and, therefore, to the extent that schooling is promoting one goal, it will be deemphasizing another. For instance, a school system that emphasizes preparing students for a world of work cannot simultaneously prepare them to be the critical thinkers called for in a democratic society. A totalitarian society can simply tell people what to think; as many have observed, independent thinking in a totalitarian society can be dangerous to one's health. In a democracy, though, one must be able to critique and evaluate information for its veracity, rejecting those who cannot provide sufficient warrant for their claims. Those concerned with individual liberties have distorted the purposes of such work-oriented aspects of some education reforms, such as "lifelong learning," seeing them, in at least one instance, as directly come to us from Chinese communist society. There is no doubt, though, reading many of the job-oriented reform documents, that part of what is desired is an expert and skilled workforce, yes, but also a docile one.

When Dwight Eisenhower left office, he warned us of a "military-industrial complex" that could subvert democracy. If he were around today, he would no doubt warn of a "government-industrial complex" in which the needs of the people are subordinated to the needs of industry and in which all human interaction is reduced to a commercial exchange. This is part of "A Nation At Risk's" legacy.

"A Nation At Risk" did not address the issue of school choice, but it has served as powerful rhetoric to those advocating giving people some say in where their children go to school. In addition, as part of a strategy of softening up the public to permit the transfer of public funds to private institutions, the Reagan and Bush administrations refused to say anything good about American public schools and accentuated anything that cast them in a negative light.

> *When a large, federally funded report concluded that there was no crisis in Amercian education, the Bush administration suppressed it.*

Thus, when a large, federally funded report concluded that there was no crisis in American education, the Bush administration suppressed it.[13]

Thus, when an international comparison of mathematics and science appeared to show American students performing poorly (the U.S. ranks were mostly low, but the students performance was quite average[14]), a press conference was called and the results received wide play from both print and electronic media. On the other hand, when an international comparison of reading skills in thirty-one nations found American students second in the world and found the best U.S. readers—the 90th, 95th, and 99th percentiles—outscoring all countries, no attempt was made to tell anyone and not one media outlet carried the results. The study was eventually discovered by *Education Week,* which carried it on page 1. Even then, only one other media source, *USA Today,* played off of *Education Week's* story. And the *USA Today* article carried a quote from a Deputy Assistant Secretary of Education dismissing the study.

Similarly, following "Risk" there was a lot of sentiment among high education officials that teachers were at fault. After all, everyone knew that high school seniors who said they intended to major in education had lower SAT scores than those for other intended majors. The U.S. Department of Education commissioned a study to document the stupidity of the teaching corps. However, the study showed that teachers-to-be have college grade point averages as high as any other major in the first two years of college—before they start to take the reputedly grade-inflated education courses. The study was never published.

Engineers at Sandia National Laboratories conducted a large, systematic study of the U.S. educational system and concluded that while the system had problems, it was not in crisis and that, indeed, it was performing much better than people thought. The study was suppressed. The official reason given was that it was undergoing "peer review." As Daniel Tanner pointed out, however, such "peer review" of one U.S. Department by others was unprecedented.[15] I saw two of the reviews, one from the National Science Foundation and one from the U.S. Department of Education, and can report that both were patently political in their criticisms. The "Sandia Report," as it came to be known, was completed in late 1990 but never published before the Bush administration was replaced (although it was widely circulated by those who found out about it). As mentioned in endnote 13, it eventually saw print as the entirety of the May/June 1993 issue of the *Journal of Educational Research.*

There have also been deliberate attempts to mislead Americans about their schools. In 1993, William Bennett released numbers purporting to show that there is no relationship between state-level SAT scores and money spent on education. This report was widely disseminated by the Heritage Foundation and the table displaying the numbers was reproduced in the *Wall Street Journal.* The Heritage Foundation's *Candidate's Handbook, 1996* reproduced the numbers once again. Yet, people, including

Bennett, have known for years that the principal source of differences among states is the proportion of seniors taking the SAT. In Utah and Mississippi, only 4 percent of the seniors take the test, and this tiny elite does well. In Connecticut, 82 percent of the senior class huddles in angst on Saturday mornings to bubble in answer sheets. With four-fifths of its senior class taking the test, Connecticut is digging much deeper into its talent pool, and that excavation shows up in lower scores.

Bennett knew that the SAT was not a test that could be used across all states. When he was Secretary of Education, he released annual charts ranking states on a variety of indicators. But those charts divided the states into two categories before any rankings were made: states that used the SAT and states that used the other college entrance test battery, the ACT. When it comes to reporting educational data, the compiler of *The Book of Virtues* has been quite willing to ignore two of them: truth and honesty.

Why would people deliberately attempt to put the worst possible face on American education? Well, some critics truly believe that a free market system would improve schools. (There is little actual evidence that this might happen; results from the British choice system indicate that the negative outcomes outweigh the positives; results from the only U.S. program that was adequately evaluated concluded that public school students actually outperformed those who were sent by the program to private schools.[16]) There are those, both with Catholic school backgrounds and with fundamentalist affiliations, who would like to see private religious schools receive public funds without the usual proscription against teaching religion or engaging in religious practices. From the nineteenth century on, business and industry have tried to control the curriculum and purpose of schools to produce docile and cheap workers. And, finally, there are those who see the public school system as one of the few remaining untapped markets, as a place to make enormous profits. The social consequences be damned.

The constant stream of negativity has created a climate in which the media accentuate the negative and even make errors because numbers, although false, corroborate what we all know is wrong. For instance, in the February 10 issue in 1993, the usually reliable *Education Week* conducted a ten-year retrospective on what had happened since "A Nation At Risk" appeared. The answer, essentially, was "not much." The paper reported that the "proportion of high school students who perform at high levels remains infinitesimally small. For instance, in the last decade the number and proportion of students scoring above 650 on the SAT verbal and mathematics test has declined." In a box next to the text, the paper put the numbers that confirmed the fall. But a close check revealed that while the numbers for 1982 were accurate, the numbers for 1992 were only for students scoring between 650 and 690, omitting all of the students between 700 and 800, the maximum SAT score. When those were added in, the numbers scoring above 650 rose for both tests and the proportion for mathematics attained a record high. In the next years, the proportion of high scorers continued to rise. Heritage Foundation fellow Denis Doyle, writing in *The Candidate's Handbook, 1996*, ascribed the growth to the performance of Asian-American students. It is true that Asian-American students do score much higher on the SAT-M than other ethnic groups, but they account for far too few test takers to cause much of the growth. In fact, there has been a 74 percent increase in the proportion of students scoring above 650 since 1981. If one omits Asian students from the sample, one still sees a 57 percent increase from 1981 to 1995.[17]

In late 1996, most of the statistics indicate the same thing that Silberman found twenty-five years earlier. The data favor "now" over "then": Achievement test scores are at record levels, and the number of students taking Advanced Placement examinations has been soaring, even as the number of students declined each year after the Baby Boom passed through. Seven of the nine trends in reading, mathematics, and science of the National Assessment of Educational Progress are at all-time highs. If the demographic changes in who takes the SAT are factored out, there remains only a small decline in the verbal score and none at all in mathematics. As noted earlier, the proportion of students scoring above 650 on the SAT mathematics test is at an all-time high and U.S. students are near the top in reading and average in mathematics and science.[18]

The biggest threat to the U.S. educational system comes from those who, for various reasons, advocate the privatization of schools. These have mostly retreated from the grand plans envisioned by Reagan and Bush. They have jumped on the latest educational bandwagon—charter schools—in hopes of using them as Trojan horses for larger choice programs in the future.

The preceding paragraph, which closed the original article, is now obsolete, although the first sentence certainly remains true. Voucher referenda in California and Michigan were soundly defeated, 70 to 30 percent in the 2000 elections. The 2002 elections, though, brought vouchers back to the fore in several states. Vouchers were part of the original No Child Left Behind legislation, and Bush has put $75 million in his fiscal 2004 budget to promote a voucher program in Washington, D.C. Some congressmen want to see it in other cities, as well. This essay provides a history. For a projection to the future, see Chapter 1, "The No Child Left Behind Act, a Plan for the Destruction of Public Education."

Notes

1. Ralph Tyler, *Perspectives on American Education: Reflections on the Past, Challenges for the Future.* Chicage, IL: Science Research Associates, 1976.

2. Raymond E. Callahan. *Education and the Cult of Efficiency.* Chicago, IL: University of Chicago Press, 1962, p. 116.

3. Lawrence J. Cremin, *Popular Education and Its Discontents.* New York: Harper & Row, 1989, pp. 102–103.

4. U.S. Office of Education, 1945, quoted in Arthur Bestor, *Educational Wastelands: The Retreat from Learning in Public Schools.* Champaign, IL: University of Illinois Press, 1953, p. 82.

5. Hyman G. Rickover, *Education and Freedom.* New York: E. P. Dutton, 1959.

6. Sloan Wilson, "It's Time to Close Our Circus." *Life,* March 24, 1958, pp. 36–37.

7. The Scholastic Aptitude Test was actually developed in 1926. In 1941, it took its modern form, and the scores from that year were a fixed standard until 1995. The 10,654 students who set the standard were an elite: 98 percent white, 60 percent male, and 40 percent from private college preparatory high schools. Most had their sights on Ivy League or Seven Sisters colleges or similar New England institutions.

8. Joseph Featherstone, "How Children Learn." *New Republic,* September 2, 1967; "Schools for Children: What's Happening in British Classrooms?" *New Republic,* August 19, 1967; "Teaching Children to Think." *New Republic,* September 9, 1967. "Open education" was a complex development originally intended only for ages 5 to 7. The phrase, as used in England, referred to attempts to develop challenging learning situations in more informal settings than those that consti- tuted the typical classroom. In the United States, the *open* in open edu- cation quickly became confused with open space. In addition, the practices were extended first to all elementary grades, then into high school, with little or no research to support such expansions. The inevitable result was that open education became another in a long line of education fads and faded from view about seven years after being introduced.

9. This assertion is not true for developing countries. See note 3.

10. *Education Week,* June 15, 1994.

11. The economic cycles have led people away from claiming the tight link between schools and the economy. They have not stopped cri- tiquing the schools. Now, though, the critiques come as vague warn- ings. Various CEOs have taken to the op-ed pages of the *New York Times, Washington Post* and *USA Today* to predict that if schools don't shape up, it will somehow cost us in some unspecified future time. The title of an hysterical report captured the tenor well: *Before It's Too Late.* In the text of the report, this phrase appears not only in italics, but also in red ink.

12. Thomas Jefferson, "Plan for the More General Diffusion of Knowledge," 1782.

13. The report, containing almost ninety graphs and accompanying documentation, was compiled by engineers at Sandia National labora- tories in 1990. It was ultimately published after the Clinton adminis- tration arrived under the title "Perspectives on American Education," and occupying the entirety of the May/June 1993 issue of the *Journal of Educational Research.*

14. Ranks obscure performance. When the races were run in Atlanta in the Olympics, someone always *ranked* last even though his or her *per- formance* was among the best in the world. In addition, in the interna- tional comparisons of education studies, most countries are tightly bunched in terms of performance so that small changes in performance lead to big changes in ranks. For instance, American thirteen-year-olds ranked 13th of fifteen nations, with a score of 67 percent correct. Had they managed to get only 5 percent more correct, they would have

jumped to fifth. Conversely, American nine-year-olds ranked third in science among ten nations, with a score of 65 percent correct. Had they only attained 60 percent correct, they would have fallen to 8th.

15. Daniel Tanner, "A Nation 'Truly' At Risk," *Phi Delta Kappan,* December 1993, pp. 288–97.

16. Kathryn Stearns, "School Choice: Survival of the Fittest." *Washington Post,* November 25, 1995, p. A25. John F. Wille, Troy D. Sterr, and Christopher A. Thorn, *Fifth Year Report: Milwaukee Parental Choice Program.* Madison WI: Department of Political Science, University of Wisconsin, December 1995.

17. The proportion of high scorers continued to rise each year through 2002, the most recent year for which data are available.

18. This paragraph remains true in 2003, although scores on one test, the Iowa Tests of Basic Skills, have declined slightly.

18   Filet of School Reform, Sauce Diable

Education's failure to make progress in comparison to the advances of other enterprises has caused much commentary in the last decades. Rampant, perseverating Taylorism seems to be the current favorite explanation. I submit there is another reason: a pathological failure to adopt good practice. I call it the pathology of envy.

This idea came to me over a dinner in Cleveland, and because of it. The linking of supper and schools in my head is not as surprising as some might think: I have written many more articles about food, wine, and restaurants in the last decade than about education. Education and edibles are often intertwined in my thoughts (causing indigestion on occasion).

> We have made less progress in education than in cooking in part because a pathology of envy prevents good education ideas from becoming widespread.

The revelatory meal in question was served in a chain hotel and consisted of lobster ravioli in an herbed cream sauce, followed by medallions of lamb "Wellington": four noisettes, each coated with Stilton cheese and spinach, then wrapped in pastry. Around the edge of the plate lay red potatoes cut in the shape of mushroom halves; in the center, cauliflower and broccoli florettes surrounded a carrot puree. The entire ensemble was floated on a thick sauce poivrade. The concoction represented an interesting mix of classic and nouvelle influences.

In a regular-sized beef Wellington, it is easy to render the pastry flaky while leaving the meat rare, but to accomplish that with this miniature rendition posed the chef quite a challenge. He/she did not rise to it fully, choosing to leave the dough a little limp in order to preserve some redness in the meat.

What struck me about this dish, though, was not that a number of kitchens in our culinary capitals could have executed it better, although that is certainly true, but that twenty-five years ago, probably no more than a dozen establishments in the entire country could have brought it off in the first place. Twenty-five years ago, I figure, probably La Bourgogne, Ernie's, and the Blue Fox in San Francisco and La Cote Basque, La Caravelle, Lafayette, and La Grenouille in New York City could have done it.

Consider that in 1968 Julia Child's *Mastering the Art of French Cooking* was only two years old (trivia challenge: name the other two authors). In 1968 Harry Reasoner dined with the *New York Times'* restaurant critic, Craig Claiborne, on *60 Minutes* and asked how Mr. Claiborne knew that the veal they were munching was top-notch. Mr. Claiborne disclosed the deep secret that good veal cooks up white, while mediocre veal turns grey. What a revelation. In 1968, "hotel food" was an oxymoron.

> *A quarter of a century after Julia Child's first book alta cucina and haute cuisine in the heart of our meat-and-potatoes Rust Belt are routine.*

Now, a quarter of a century later, alta cucina and haute cuisine in the heart of our meat-and-potatoes Rust Belt is routine. A classroom of 1993, we are told, though, still looks like a classroom of 1968. How come?

Well, consider this incident. In September 1991, the cover of *N.E.A. Today* carried a picture of Indianapolis' Key School, and the question "Is this the best elementary school in the country?" A few weeks later, I called Pat Bolaños, the principal of the Key School, whom I have known since 1986, and asked her what the reaction had been to the article. "Not as bad as I had expected," she said.

Not as bad as I had expected? If a new restaurant gets raves, everyone beats a path to its door—including other chefs. The best cooks are always checking out others' creations and techniques. Some leading restaurateurs I've known would take their whole kitchens to visit places of repute, then hold seminars on what they had found. My favorite chef in Denver annually jets to either France or Italy to see what's new and to study with a peer. This emulation writ large has changed us overnight from a nation of pot roasts to one of polpettone.

But when it comes to adopting good pedagogical practice, school folk exhibit a pathology of envy. It takes several forms. The most common may be stated as, "If you have a new idea, I'd better get one, too, but it can't be yours." This leads to a hypercompetition among schools, especially among elementary principals, but not to a search for best practice—only for something new to do. Or appear to do.

It also takes the form, "If you've got a good idea, keep it to yourself. Otherwise, I'll look bad." Some negative reactions to the *N.E.A. Today* article on the Key School occurred precisely because the magazine was making a good idea more public.

The Key School, a magnet school to which students are admitted by lottery and who match the ethnic mix of the city as a whole, is organized mostly around the notions of multiple intelligences laid out by Howard Gardner in *Frames of Mind*. Everyone learns a foreign language, everyone learns a musical instrument (daily instruction in both). Instruction emphasizes fine arts and computers. The teachers follow a theme-based curriculum that they develop and also teach subjects that interest them outside of school (for instance, pottery making or Victorian architecture). A "flow center," developed from Mihaly Csikszentmihali's concept of flow, helps determine what really turns kids on. On Wednesday afternoons, the teachers gather for a planning meeting while the students congregate in the gym/auditorium and listen to and ask questions of some group from the community (paramedics, symphony musicians, etc.). Most children find most elementary schools hospitable, but the Key School's students seem even happier to be there than at most other places I have visited.

The Key School has received adoring attention from the press, the networks, and PBS. One would think, therefore, that other educators would stampede to adopt and adapt its principles and practices. This is not, after all, a hothouse experiment operating under some visionary's unique set of notions in a no-fail, affluent neighborhood. It is a public school in a working-class setting developed by a group of public school teachers that Mr. Gardner once referred to as "plain vanilla." It ought to be possible to make a Key School anywhere, and people ought to be building Key Schools around the country.

> *It ought to be possible to make a Key School anywhere, and people ought to be building Key Schools around the country.*

Not so. Indeed, one year when I visited the school, I met teachers who were interested in making a Key middle school.[1] At least, they were interested now. "Before we actually came to the Key School, we had all kinds of misinformation about it," said one. "I thought it was a school for gifted and talented students," said another. "I thought it got results only because of its extra planning periods," said a third. "I hated the Key School," said yet another.

Hated the Key School? Had all kinds of misinformation about it? Why isn't the district getting the word out to other buildings? I don't know, but offhand, I also don't know of any district that has a mechanism for such dissemination.

It would be nice if we could write off the ignoring of the Key School as an exception. Alas, it is the rule. Deborah Meier of the much-lauded Central Park East Secondary School in New York City reports similar disinterest. If interest in model practice were high, Edward Fiske's *Smart Kids, Smart Schools* would have climbed the best-seller charts.

Ironically, programs that are developed by persons external to any public school have a much easier time gaining wide access. Entrepreneurial educational ventures sweep across the land quickly, although they often disappear as the next fad looms on the horizon—or when the data about their efficacy actually begin to arrive. But a program or an idea developed by school people and used in a real school has little chance of affecting even its most immediate neighbors. Or, perhaps we should say, *especially* its most immediate neighbors.

As long as this pathology of envy endures, it is not likely that all the frenzy of "restructuring" and "empowerment" and site-based management is going to accomplish nearly as much as it might if the empowered, restructured sites adopted good models of what to teach, how, when, and to whom. The principal of each school ought to take his/her whole staff out to a good restaurant and cogitate on this problem over a creme brulee and cognac.

Note

1. This school has been in existence for some years now and was developed largely at the request of graduates of the Key elementary school who reported back that they were "dying" in traditional middle schools. On 1999, the Key School began adding one high school grade per year, and their first class graduated in 2003.

19. Edison's Light Dims
The Rise and Fall and Rise and Fall of H. Christopher Whittle

S ummer 2001 was shaping up nicely for H. Christopher Whittle and his company, Edison Schools Inc. After ten consecutive years in the red, the nation's largest publicly traded, for-profit Education Management Organization seemed poised to deliver a return on investment.

Black ink at the bottom line would go a long way to refute skeptics who thought his "revolutionary educational model" promised too much to be profitable. Announcing the project in 1991, Whittle vowed that students in his schools would learn to read from classic books, not basal readers. By the time they left Edison, *all* students would have consumed Advanced Placement Calculus or a college-level course in probability and statistics (currently, about 7 percent of American high school students take calculus). They would learn science through cooperative, project-based learning, not books. Edison would put computers in their homes as well as in their schools. The Internet would connect the computers and students to experts all over the country who would evaluate the student projects.

All this left some observers breathless and with eyebrows raised, but Whittle was not finished: Edison would bring the revolution for free. That is, Edison schools would cost no more than what the typical public school district spent for each child. Thomas Alva Edison, said Whittle, didn't build a better candle. He invented a new way of generating light. Just so with Edison schools. But by 2001 Edison had lost money every single quarter of its existence, and Edison's light was dimming.

Only a few months earlier, Spring 2001 had looked promising, but March turned out to be the cruelest month. New York City Public Schools Chancellor Harold Levy wanted Edison to manage five of his lowest performing schools. Although five schools didn't constitute a large contract, the schools were, after all, in New York. Five New York City schools would be a public relations coup in a way that five schools in any other city could not be. "If we do a great job in these schools, we believe there will be more schools headed our way," Whittle told the *New York Times*.

Levy's orchestration of the takeover favored Edison. While the law required that Levy put the contract out on bid, his criteria for eligibility excluded every potential bidder save Edison. Levy's plan, though, contained a fatal (for Edison) flaw. The proposal required that the parents of children in the affected schools vote on it. For Edison to take over the schools, 50 percent of the parents had to say "yes."

Initially, Levy tapped Edison not only to send out information about the vote, but to conduct the vote itself. Community groups howled and Levy yielded, permitting them to circulate anti-Edison materials. Parents voted 4–1 against. Even the school considered most likely to ask Edison in tallied only 36 percent yes votes. Whittle's star turn in the Big Apple had been canceled in rehearsal.

But now came Tom Ridge in the summer, still governor of Pennsylvania. In the first week of August, he bestowed upon Edison a $2.7 million no-bid contract to "study" the Philadelphia school system and recommend how to "fix" it. To some observers, the district did not appear to be broken, merely starved by the state funding formula. People cried conflict of interest over letting Edison "study" a system it no doubt wanted to manage.

Observers expected Edison to recommend that Edison take over the district. Edison did not disappoint. It concluded that Philadelphia's schools could best be fixed by replacing fifty-five top administrators with Edison appointees and by hiring Edison to directly manage forty-five low-performing schools. The resulting contract would bring Edison $300 million dollars over a three-year span. Surely such a windfall would send the company into the black.

Harrisburg versus Philadelphia

Whittle had courted other governors, including Lamar Alexander of Tennessee, William Weld of Massachusetts, and George W. Bush of Texas. It seems reasonable, then, that in wooing Ridge, he knew he was stepping into the long history of hostility between Harrisburg and Philadelphia. Philadelphia is liberal and Democratic. Harrisburg is not. Harrisburg caters to the state's overwhelmingly rural population. Philadelphia does not. (Pennsylvania is Philadelphia and Pittsburgh at the edges and Alabama in between, goes an old Keystone State saying.)

For many years, while Harrisburg officially housed the state government, the cultural capital resided in Philadelphia. As Philadelphia's wealth declined and its minority populations increased, ethnic and poverty-related strains emerged (currently, 80 percent of Philadelphia's school children are black or Hispanic). The legislature changed the school funding formula in 1991 and hurt Philadelphia badly. The city's schools sank from surpluses into deficits. With difficulties mounting, in 1994 the city appointed David Hornbeck superintendent. Hornbeck had been Pennsylvania Secretary of Education from 1972 to 1976, and his subsequent work in Maryland and Kentucky had earned him a reputation for intelligence, innovation, and contentiousness.

As the school system's financial plight worsened, so did antagonisms between Ridge and Hornbeck. State funding levels forced Hornbeck to send out hundreds of layoff notices. In 1996, he swore that he would never cut a budget again. Ridge, for his part, said, "I've got 500 school superintendents who are willing to live within their means and one who is not." Ridge apparently did not notice—or did not care—that Philadelphia's means were already smaller than those in the surrounding suburban districts and were dwindling.

In 1998, faced with even more red ink, Hornbeck angered Ridge, and some legislators, by filing suits in federal court. First came an equity suit, then a second suit that charged that the state's funding formula discriminated against blacks. Some legislators became enraged, feeling that Hornbeck had called *them* racists. When I asked about this, Hornbeck said, "I never called anyone a racist. The funding system is racist, though, because it discriminates against black kids."

Although he probably did not know it at the time, Hornbeck was about to lose some vital support in the city government. When his contract came up for renewal in 1999, his Board enthusiastically supported a two-year reappointment. The City Council was not so eager. Fifteen Council members wrote the Board of Education, asking it to limit Hornbeck's extension to one year. A mayoral election was in the offing. The Council sensed that Council President John Street, Mayor Ed Rendell's choice to succeed him, would not have the same relationship with Hornbeck that Rendell had enjoyed.

For one thing, although he had agreed to it, Street had reservations about the "trainwreck scenario" concocted by Rendell and Hornbeck. Under this plan, they would start new school programs as if the state had appropriated the money. They would reduce class size in grades 1 through 3 and extend kindergarten from half-day to all day. When the money ran out, as they anticipated it would in March of the coming year, they would simply shut the schools down. Trainwreck. Street would have preferred to try to work things out with the governor and the legislature. Extending Hornbeck's superintendency only one year instead of two would allow the new mayor, whomever it might be, to name his own person.

Largely because of last minute stumping by President Clinton, Street did become mayor. Differences between Street and Hornbeck surfaced almost immediately. Street proposed that the state, which already ran the city's finances, take over the district's as well. In return, Street expected increased funding for small classes, higher teacher salaries and badly needed school repairs. Hornbeck opposed any state intervention in the district's affairs.

Street persuaded the Board to trim $30 million from the budget and to postpone Hornbeck's suit. At the time, George W. Bush already looked to have the 2000 Republican presidential nomination cinched, and Ridge's name was floating as a potential running mate. The suit and a state takeover of the schools would both produce political nastiness and diminish his chances. Street's actions soothed Ridge. Hornbeck quit.

When Bush tapped Dick Cheney as his vice presidential running mate, he freed Ridge to pursue his Philadelphia problem as he chose. He chose Edison.

To a lot of people, Edison was an odd choice. For starters, people wondered about the logic of giving a debt-ridden district to a money-losing company. Edison had come to Ridge's attention through his secretary of education, Eugene Hickok, and an adviser, Charles Zogby. (In 2001, Hickok had departed to be Deputy Secretary of Education for Bush, and Zogby had replaced him.) Hickok had been active in the Education Leadership Council, a group of conservative education reformers on chummy terms with Edison. He and Zogby had also sat on a commission that oversaw an earlier state takeover in nearby Chester Upland District. The commission delivered Chester Upland to Edison.

> To a lot of people, Edison was an odd choice. People wondered about the logic of the choice giving a debt-ridden district to a money-losing company.

Thus, in the summer of 2001 Ridge awarded Edison the $2.7 million to study the system. Edison's rapid response raised even more eyebrows. To collect and analyze the data to evaluate a 210,000-student district, Edison, which had never conducted such a study and had no real expertise to do so, needed only two months. By contrast, the RAND Corporation, a research think tank with a long track record and a reputation for fairness, will require four years to complete its study of Edison.

The hastily assembled report might have satisfied the folks in Harrisburg, but more objective reviewers panned it. The Council of the Great City Schools found that it "contains a number of factual errors" and "uses weak techniques and questionable assumptions" to reach its conclusions. And those conclusions "appear to have been reached before any data were analyzed or any interviews conducted." Edison's wording of opinion-survey questions guaranteed that the schools would appear in the worst possible light.

Fall 2001 saw a series of confrontations between Mark Schweiker, now governor after Ridge departed to head up Homeland Security, and Street. But, somehow, in closed talks, the white Republican governor and the African American Democratic mayor managed to reach an agreement in November and clinched the deal on December 21.

The Schweiker-Street agreement included the appointment of a School Reform Commission (SRC) to oversee the takeover. Schweiker's choice to head the SRC was a Philadelphia business executive, James Nevels. Nevels had earlier sat with Hickok and Zogby on the commission that awarded Chester Upland schools to Edison. In addition to having his man chair the group, Schweiker had Street outvoted if any contentious issues arose. He had three SRC appointments, and Street had two. The SRC looked like a ploy to let Schweiker give the district to Edison without actually taking responsibility for the deal.

Nevels surprised people by not contracting immediately with Edison, but by sending out requests for proposals and obtaining bids from twenty-two companies in early 2002. On April 17, the SRC announced that seventy schools would undergo major reforms. The district would convert four to charter school status, permit teachers and parents to run five as "independent" schools, and "reconstitute" nineteen, meaning that their teacher faculties could be replaced. Several private companies similar to Edison would manage some of the schools.

The SRC reached all of these decisions with unanimous votes. No one on the SRC voted to give Edison the forty-five schools it had asked for. The three Schweiker appointees thought Edison deserved twenty schools. Street's people argued that Edison lacked the expertise to handle so many schools at once (most Edison contracts were for two to four schools). They favored awarding Edison only six. On a 3–2 vote, Edison got the twenty.

Although twenty schools were more than twice as many as in any other Edison operation, Edison's failure to obtain the forty-five it sought disappointed investors. Since Whittle had taken the company public in 1999, creditors and investors alike had shrugged off his profitless history. No more. Whittle had assured investors that Edison would capture contracts in both New York and Philadelphia. Wall Street saw Edison as 0 for 2.

Edison's initial public offering in 1999 had come in at $16 a share. The stock had risen as high as $39, then drifted back to $18, tumbling to $12 after New York City parents rejected Edison's proposed takeover there. Now it plummeted, dipping below the dollar mark on May 29. On June 4, it rallied to $1.61

on the news that Whittle had cobbled together the $40 million in credit he needed to start the Philadelphia operation, but it soon slipped back below a dollar and as fall 2002 arrived, hovered around 30 cents, with delisting from the NASDAQ threatened.

Coming on the heels of the New York debacle, the Philadelphia shock brought Edison's shares to the penny-stock level, but just after that disappointment, Edison found itself buffeted by bad news from all over. While the Enron, WorldCom, and Arthur Andersen scandals were still garnering headlines, Edison revealed that it, too, had been investigated by the Securities and Exchange Commission for its creative accounting procedures. Worse, it had kept the investigation secret for three months. The SEC found Edison's revenues overstated by 41 percent and compelled Edison to change its accounting procedures. Three law firms filed class action suits charging "Edison Schools, Inc. and certain of its officers and directors with issuing false and misleading statements concerning its business and financial condition."

The stock collapse also meant the end of easy credit. Edison needed $40 million to start its Philadelphia operations. It got the dollars, but at interest rates rumored to be in the "low teens." This at a time when the prime rate was running around 5 percent.

Even Edison's association with its longtime biggest booster and creditor, Merrill Lynch, suddenly looked a bit unseemly. Lynch had granted Edison a $35 million line of credit in late 2001 and had ponied up another $20 million to help Edison cover its Philadelphia obligations. But now Eliot Spitzer, the New York Attorney General, accused Lynch of trashing in private emails stocks it had publicly touted. (The company coughed up $100 million, while not admitting any wrongdoing.)

News arriving from various Edison campuses compounded problems. Upland District reported that in its Edison schools, suspensions, truancy warning letters, and serious violent incidents were up and attendance was down. Clarke County, Nevada (Las Vegas), schools withheld a $3 million dollar payment to Edison because of $10.5 million in unmet obligations. Dade County, Florida, also withheld payments because of unpaid bills. Inskter, Michigan, threatened to terminate its contract. The Texas Education Agency dropped its rating of two of Edison's seven Dallas schools from "acceptable" to "low achieving," stimulating the Dallas School Board to reevaluate the contract. Dallas' own evaluation found that, in spite of costing $2,000 more per child than public schools, Edison schools did no better than demographically similar publics. It cancelled its Edison contract.

In Boston, Edison's Renaissance Charter School, one of Edison's oldest and largest contracts, ended its relationship with the firm. And Mount Clemens, in Michigan, also one of Edison's original four clients, terminated its contract. Wichita axed two of four Edison schools, citing plummeting test scores, skyrocketing teacher and student turnover, and possible cheating on tests. (It has since ended all Edison contracts.) Bibb County, Georgia (Macon), also backed out.

Edison Board member and former New York City Public Schools Chancellor Ramon Cortines resigned, saying the company lacked integrity. Cortines accused Edison of always hiding bad news from the Board. As an example, Cortines mentioned an Edison report of $7.5 million in revenues for running four schools in Mount Clemens. In fact, Edison had used district services for transportation and meals and other services, and these had cost more than Edison's fees. Edison received, therefore, nothing.

Edison hurt itself by keeping the SEC investigation from the public for three months, so investors and observers were doubly stunned when, on October 1, 2002, Edison reveal another indecorous secret: Its audit committee had resigned more than two months earlier on the advice of their lawyers. NASDAQ, which had already warned Edison of a potential delisting because of its share price, requires a committee of three independent people.

In August 2002, Edison fired 211 secretaries and nonteaching assistants from its twenty Philadelphia schools. In some of its schools, foreign language and music classes have not materialized, no new computers have been delivered, and classes are short of books. Edison also returned truckloads of supplies, payment for which, said Edison spokesman Adam Tucker, was predicated on getting forty-five schools, not twenty. Philadelphia's new school CEO, Paul Vallas, filed papers to protect the schools' books, computers, and other supplies in the event of an Edison bankruptcy.

For its fourth quarter, ending June 30, 2002, Edison posted a loss of $49.3 million, or 92 cents a share, up from $11.5 million and 22 cents a share the previous year. The day after reporting the loss, Edison suspended plans for a $125 million new headquarters building in Harlem.

As the 2002 school year started, Edison struggled even more, with teachers complaining about no textbooks in some schools and none of the promised computers in others. Edison abandoned its Philadelphia headquarters and tried to set up shop in a school. Refused this, Edison's lead man in Philly repaired to a hotel while other employees scattered around the city.

In early October, CEO Vallas ripped Edison for spending $300,000 on a three-day principals' retreat at the posh Broadmoor Hotel in Colorado Springs. Whittle took much heat personally for proposing at the meeting that school children could replace adults in some basic administrative jobs. Spokesman Tucker said the comments had been taken out of context, but an undisputed account of the talk from *Bloomberg News* said Whittle proposed having the kids do "big" parts of school offices and "huge" parts of school technology systems. Edison students in Philadelphia (and elsewhere) are overwhelmingly elementary school pupils. People wondered just how much could be transferred to children age twelve and under. Community groups accused Whittle of being willing to violate child labor laws and, therefore, to be morally unfit to operate schools.

Community groups accused Whittle of being willing to violate child labor laws and, therefore, to be morally unfit to operate schools.

As October waned, Edison started buying back stock, and rumors circulated about a reverse stock split. Both actions were seen as attempts to drive up the stock's price over $1 a share and avoid delisting by NASDAQ. It worked. At Thanksgiving, the stock closed at $1.65. People who had bought at the low of 14 cents were more than willing to take a near 1200 percent profit.

Even if Edison manages to survive its legal and fiscal challenges, and gets test scores up in Philadelphia, some people in Chicago think its days there are numbered under Vallas. Vallas was previously Chicago's CEO and unsuccessful Illinois gubernatorial candidate. Vallas lost his school post in part because of friction between himself and another mammoth ego, Mayor Richard Daley. Some Chicago school people hold that Philadelphia is too small a town for two prima donnas.

In addition, Edison's friends in Harrisburg are gone. Democrat Ed Rendell, the former Philadelphia mayor, replaced Schweiker as governor in 2002. For his part, Secretary of Education Zogby's zealotry on behalf of Edison raised an unusually large number of hackles. Zogby departed to become a vice president on Bill Bennett's online venture, K12, Inc.

The loss of friends in high places could augur badly for Edison. In late November, Pennsylvania's Auditor General released his audit of how Edison came by the original $2.7 million contract. The scathing report called it a sweetheart deal done behind closed doors by a few lawyers who ignored the fact that Edison had no qualifications for the study it was receiving the money to do. Worse, the state had just paid $7.5 million to a company that did have the qualifications, Standard and Poor's. S & P had evaluated every school in the state, and the Edison report added nothing. The auditor observed that the written justification for awarding Edison "recites almost verbatim the promotional information about Edison from the company's own website." He claimed the contract violated Pennsylvania law, which requires competitive bids.

The Edison Saga

Starting in 1968, Chris Whittle made his first batch of money with something called "Knoxville in a Nutshell," an ad-stuffed guide to Knoxville for students entering the University of Tennessee. With this money, he and pal Philip Moffitt bought an ailing *Esquire* magazine in 1979. With Moffitt carrying most of the editorial load and Whittle charming advertisers, they turned the publication around. Their successes were such that four years later, they celebrated *Esquire's* fiftieth anniversary with a black tie celebration for which they rented Avery Fisher Hall at Lincoln Center. In 1986, they sold *Esquire* to Hearst.

The exuberant Whittle and the introspective Moffitt had always made a strange couple; now they split. Yoga devotee Moffitt took up Jungian psychology. Whittle founded Whittle Communications, Inc., and launched large projects. Time, Inc. invested $185,000, and Phillips Consumer Electric, $80 million. Whittle bought a $12 million house on Manhattan's East Side and a sixteen acre estate in East Hampton, ocean view. (In the fall of 2002, Whittle put this mansion on the market for $45 million and sold it to clothing tycoon, Tommy Hilfiger, reportedly for $31 million.)

Whittles' ventures mostly wobbled. Medical News Network had development costs of $100 million. It never recovered them. Special Reports, was initially profitable, but never had the 100 million readers Whittle claimed in full-page ads in the *New York Times* and soon sputtered. Channel One, the best known of these undertakings, beamed twelve-minute "newscasts" laced with two minutes of ads into public school classes.

Although initially successful, Channel One failed to gain access to New York and California and soon faced growing dissatisfaction in Texas, its largest market. Evaluations of Channel One concluded that children didn't learn anything from the newscasts, which were much shorter than promised. They did learn from the ads, which were much longer than promised. Although the ads were mostly for junk foods, children assumed that, because they viewed them in their classrooms, the products must be good for them.

> *Although Channel One's ads were mostly for junk foods, children assumed that, because they viewed them in their classrooms, the products must be good for them.*

When it came to light that Whittle had used creative accounting to exaggerate income and had failed to pay property taxes on his hundreds of thousands of television sets, Jay Johnstone was brought in as CEO from Philips and liquidated the company. KIII Communications bought it for $300 million. Time and Philips wrote off their investments.

With Channel One, Special Report, and Medical News Network behind him, Whittle now turned his attention to salvaging the one "asset" he had managed to hang on to, the money-losing Edison Project. In 1991, with customary optimism and bravado, Whittle proclaimed that his Edison Schools would revolutionize education. And not cost anything. "We believe we can do all this spending the same amount per student as the average school district now spends," wrote Edison president, and former Yale University president, Benno Schmidt. Neither Schmidt, nor virtually anyone involved in Edison's start-up, had any experience with public schools.

Whittle estimated that it would take $2.5 billion to fulfill his vision of two hundred private schools by 1996, and one thousand by 2000. Time-Warner declined to sign on. Disney, Paramount Communications, and TeleCommunications, Inc. also spurned Whittle's advances. Whittle did manage to cajole yet another $40 million out of big Channel One loser, Philips Electronics.

It was a risky venture from the start, but no one seemed to ask hard questions about it—like, who would send their children to Whittle's private schools? Few people with children already in private schools were likely to be enticed out of them. Few people in the suburbs, satisfied with the public schools they found there, were likely to fork out a sizable sum for some start-up private school company. And poor people didn't have money for tuition.

In fact, Whittle's scheme depended on the political fortunes of George H. W. Bush and Lamar Alexander. Whittle had hired Alexander as a consultant when Alexander was governor of Tennessee. When Alexander became president of the University of Tennessee, Whittle put him on the Board of Whittle Communications. Whittle sold Alexander Whittle Communications stock for $10,000, and bought it back for $330,000 without, apparently, ever cashing Alexander's original check. At the moment of Edison's inception, Republicans were already mentioning Alexander as a presidential contender. (He would run five years later.)

In 1991 Alexander was Secretary of Education to George H. W. Bush. Bush, riding record-high popularity ratings after the Gulf War, was considered a shoo-in for reelection in 1992. Bush and Alexander advocated school vouchers, a concept introduced to the White House by Bush's predecessor, Ronald Reagan.

Under a voucher system, money for schooling would not go to the schools, but would go directly to families in the form of vouchers. Families could use the vouchers at any school that accepted them. Whittle's schools would. If Bush and Alexander could get voucher legislation through Congress, kids with vouchers would constitute an immediate, large pool of students with the means to attend Edison schools.

But Bill Clinton's surprise victory left Whittle without his Washington patrons and no easy means of attracting public school students to his private schools. Suburban parents weren't interested. Henry Levin of Columbia University says that Edison courted twenty schools for every one it eventually contracted with. Instead of developing a large empire of private schools, he had to accept a humbling smaller number of public schools—four—that he could only manage, not own. Increasingly, schools that yielded to Edison's entreaties were in low-income neighborhoods, not middle-class areas that Whittle had envisioned. Whittle had projected one thousand private schools by 2000, but by 2002, it managed, not owned, only 150 (123 if one uses conventional counting methods, which Edison does not), containing 80,000 students.

In these schools, Edison has never delivered on its promise of high-tech, high-performance schools at no increase above public school expense. Edison schools invariably cost more. In California, Edison found that it could not even operate without a $25 million gift from the Gap founders, Don and Doris Fisher. (In return, their D2F2 Foundation received Edison stock options that it sold for a profit.) In Philadelphia, Edison asked for an additional $1,500 per pupil for the twenty schools it runs. Dallas Associate Superintendent William Webster told me that Edison schools there cost $2,000 more per student per year. When districts have cancelled contracts, cost is always one reason cited.

Janice Solkov gave Edison's costs game away, probably in all innocence, in a *Washington Post* article.[1] Solkov had signed on in Philadelphia as the principal of an Edison school, but by Thanksgiving she was so frazzled she quit. In her article, she complained that because the SRC ad not given Edison the extra $1,800 per pupil it had asked for the "full [Edison] model could no be implemented." Eighteen hundred dollars per student would come to roughly $1 million per school. In Philadelphia, Edison had given up any pretense that it could run its schools for no more than what it cost the districts to run theirs.

Vallas had promised to halve the extra amount Edison and other private operations get. Edison has not yet reacted to Vallas' vow.

In fact, Edison has not delivered on any of the promises in its glowing 1994 planning document. This is hardly to say that Whittle and other officers have not themselves made money. In 2001, Whittle agreed to work for $1 a year plus stock options, even as the nation was concluding that options reward CEOs for all the wrong things. Earlier, though, he had received $300,000 a year plus 100,000 shares in stock options. If he cashed the shares, Edison would cover the IRS tab. In the days leading up to the New

York City debacle, he exercised some options and collected $16 million.

Over a number of years, Edison also paid a privately held Tennessee corporation, WSI, Inc., $1,848,742 and 3,098,403 shares of the company. The president and sole employee of WSI is H. Christopher Whittle.

But Does It Work?

Whittle could probably ignore criticism of his accounting practices and lavish life-style, and even the extra money it takes to run Edison schools, if he could show that the Edison "model" has accomplished anything close to what Whittle promised or, failing that, if he at least sent some money to his investors.

Alas, the numbers that Edison reports about its effectiveness have about the same credibility as those in weight-loss infomercials. Edison overstates everything, starting with the number of schools it manages. Growth is important for Edison's image, so it maximizes that number. If one building contains grades K–12, conventional counting calls that one school. Edison calls it three: an elementary, a middle, and a high. While Edison was claiming 137 schools, others were counting 109, and only 100 if the schools acquired in a 2001 purchase of the company LearnNow were excluded. Edison's September 30, 2002, filing of form 10-K with the SEC lists 26 schools in Philadelphia. Everyone else says 20.

When it comes to test scores, Edison both inflates numbers and rejects every common method of evaluating test results. Edison officers have apparently not realized that the logic Edison uses to dismiss others' evaluations also invalidates its own.

Comparing one schools' performance is not easy. Schools differ on lots of factors that affect test scores: parental wealth, parental education level, language spoken at home, and so forth. One common method is to compare the test scores of one school (or group) to those of demographically similar schools. Such comparisons form the heart of the statewide accountability procedures in both California and Texas, and it does make sense to compare like with like.

Edison rejects this type of comparison. Its *Fourth Annual Report on School Performance* issued in September 2001 claims, "A statistician would not compare the achievement of the Edison school and other schools as if each school were performing independently." That's because, Edison contends, Edison schools influence other district schools. Yet, the lore of American schools includes many stories about their insularity from other schools. And Edison mentions Edison schools in Wichita and Mount Clemens that serve as models for other schools in the district. Both districts have ended their relationships with Edison.

Edison's accountings of its schools do not agree with those of other evaluators. The Texas Education Agency demoted four Edison schools, from "acceptable" to "low achieving." Edison's report, though, still lists three of the four as "positive" for test score trends and one as "incomplete." Similarly, the California Department of Education dropped the rankings of five of eight Edison schools, all designated as positive by Edison. The other three showed slight improvements or no change in the California system.

Edison also rejects before-and-after-Edison comparisons. Again, Edison's *Fourth Annual Report:* "Schools often change their enrollments dramatically after Edison is introduced. Increased enrollments in previously under-enrolled schools are very common. Edison schools are generally schools of choice and enrollments change as families move in and out of this new program."

This is a legitimate argument, although Edison critics have attributed the changing enrollment to Edison's "counseling out" students it does not want—students with special education needs and/or low test scores. Edison schools do contain a far smaller and often declining proportion of students receiving either special education services or those characterized as English Language Learners.

Edison contends that because Edison schools "change their enrollments dramatically after Edison is introduced," this invalidates before-and-after comparisons. Yet, this argument also invalidates the one evaluation technique that Edison does accept: changes in test scores over time in the same school after Edison arrives. These "dramatic" changes in enrollments do not occur only after Edison's first year. A school that Edison has managed for five years might look very different, demographically, in year 5 than in year 1 of Edison's reign. Edison could gather valid data by tracking the *same children* as they progress through the grades, but this is something Edison does not do.

Edison often says that 84 percent of its schools show positive trends. The *New York Times* submitted Cleveland Public Schools to the same procedure Edison uses. Cleveland is one of the nation's lowest performing school systems. The *Times* found that 87.4 percent of Cleveland's schools showed "positive" test trends.

Evaluations by outside organizations have found Edison performance mixed at best. Edison has rejected all of them. Western Michigan University studied one set of schools that Edison claimed had no negative or strongly negative trends on standardized tests. According to Edison, 20 percent of the schools showed mixed trends, 30 percent were positive, and 50 percent were strongly positive. The Western Michigan researchers called 80 percent of the results "mixed." On a different set of tests, 43 percent of the trends were mixed and 47 percent were negative.[2]

> *Evaluations by outside organizations have found Edison performance mixed at best.*

In a press release Chief Edison Education Officer John Chubb, formerly of the Brookings Institution, dismissed the analysis out of hand, calling it "stunningly irresponsible. . . . The Western Michigan report is literally a scam. . . . It is shocking that social scientists would attempt to pass off such work as an objective evaluation." Chubb, a social scientist himself, and co-author of a book advocating vouchers, did not explain *how* the Western Michigan investigators had erred.

That Edison's performance should be so mediocre at best is surprising in light of some Edison program characteristics. The reading and math programs Edison uses (developed independently of Edison by educators at Johns Hopkins University and the University of Chicago, respectively) have received generally favorable evaluations. Edison students spend ninety minutes a day on reading and math each, substantially more than typical public school students. Edison schools operate both a longer school day and longer school year than do the publics. Edison students are in class fully 50 percent more hours per year than their public school peers. Why all this extra time doesn't add up to increased test scores is something of a mystery.

As for profitability, Edison has been as soft on itself as with the analysis of test score trends. In 1998, Whittle told the *Education Industry Report* that Edison schools would be very close to profitable in the fiscal year that began July 1, 1998, and that in "the year that will start July, 1999, we will make it easily." About the same time, Chief Financial Officer James L. Starr told me that the individual schools were already profitable and all that was needed was growth to realize economies of scale for administration.

In fact, Edison's obsession with growth might be part of its problem. In trying to position Edison as a growth company, Edison officers made many costly money-for-schools deals, spending more than it should have to close the deal. Once the middle-class schools failed to materialize, Edison loaned millions to charter schools in poorer neighborhoods. Parents in poor neighborhoods weren't able to help their children overcome the "digital divide" with the computers Edison donated, and Edison's staff was far too small to maintain and repair them.

Worse, the fundamental assumption Whittle made about return on investment—that rapid growth would lead to profit—appears to be wrong. Columbia's Levin argues that schools don't show an economy of scale as some businesses do, and districts become less and less efficient after they pass the six-thousand-student mark. Edison appears to be a new instance of the old joke: A company that lost money on every sale but made it up on volume.

In a May 25, 2002 editorial, the *New York Times* looked at the nature of education and found it so labor intensive that it "may never be profitable on the scale that the stock market requires." Chris Whittle could tell you all about it, except that maybe Philips' Jay Johnstone was right. As he liquidated Whittle Communications in 1994, Johnstone commented that Chris Whittle is too smart to even consider that he could be wrong. Whittle now insists that in Edison's fourth quarter, which ends June 30, 2003, the company will show its first profit.

Notes

1. Janice L. Solkov, "Privatizing Schools Just Shouldn't Be This Hard." *Washington Post,* February 2, 2004, p. B4.

2. Gary Miron and Brooks Applegate. *An Evaluation of Student Achievement in Edison Schools Opened in 1995 and 1996.* Kalamzoo, MI: The Evaluation Center, Western Michigan University, 2000.

20 Playing It Crooked
Media and Political Distortion About the Condition of American Public Schools

As part of the research that went into this chapter, I perused *The TRUTH About America's Public Schools: The Bracey Reports 1991–1997* (Bracey 1997). I rediscovered that most of those reports had a section called "The Media." I came away both depressed and cheered. Depressed because many of the problems discussed in those reports remain; cheered because at least a few things have gotten better.

On the up side, we now have the thoughtful, reasoned columns from Richard Rothstein[1] appearing every Wednesday in the *New York Times*. We also have a Houston antiques dealer putting up large numbers of newspaper articles on the Internet every day (www.educationnews.org; subscriptions are free). And we have Doug Oplinger and Dennis Willard at the *Akron Beacon Journal* conducting top-notch investigative studies of various topics in education. The Oplinger-Willard combo first described the political and fiscal machinations behind Ohio's charter school movement (Willard and Oplinger 1999a, 1999b, 1999c; Oplinger and Willard 1999a, 1999b, 1999c). More recently, they revealed how tax abatements for business and industry were costing Ohio public schools $115 million a year (Oplinger and Willard 2002). "In Ohio," they began, "business gets more tax breaks than God."

The sentence refers to the fact that businesses get more tax breaks than church-owned property. The Oplinger-Willard team is depressing as well as elating. While they provide a model of what education reporting should look like, they also show the contrast between that model and most of the rest of what's out there.

Most reporting remains shallow and short on critical analysis. A 2002 paper by Joseph Reaves at Arizona State University showed that editorials in the *New York Times, Atlanta Journal Constitution, St Louis Post-Dispatch,* and *Los Angeles Times* accepted the No Child Left Behind legislation very much as it was presented by the Bush administration. The title of Reaves' piece says a lot: "Falling in Line" (Reaves 2002). It reminded me of one commentator's criticism of the war in Iraq coverage. The commentator pointed out that the cable television channels brought on former generals, former security specialists, and others who on occasion criticized some specific tactic or strategy in the war. They produced no one who would question the Bush administration's policies or the war itself. If four of the leading newspapers in the nation aren't exercising their critical faculties (another failure of American public schools?), what can we expect from the rest?

> *Most reporting about education remains shallow and short on critical analysis.*

This problem is scarcely new. A few years ago, Richard Harwood, former *Washington Post* ombudsman, noted that "for twenty years content analysis studies have shown that 70 to 90 percent of our content is at heart the voice of officials and their experts, translated by reporters into supposedly 'objective' news" (Harwood 1994). Of course, if those officials are spinning information with a political or ideological purpose, objectivity is impossible unless the reporters go beyond the information given. For instance, a Tamara Henry piece in *USA Today* claimed that a Western Michigan University evaluation of Pennsylvania charter schools found them performing better than the public schools. Alas, Henry did not actually read the report—her article was written almost verbatim from a press release from charter enthusiast, then-governor Tom Ridge (Henry 2001). The statement was true only for the oldest charter schools—both of them.

The media's analysis deficit combined with its appetite for the negative form a potent one-two punch against schools. If it bleeds, it leads, goes the old saw. To confirm this in education, one needs only examine the placement of SAT stories each year when the College Board releases the latest scores. Downturns get page 1 treatment, while gains are either ignored, buried deep in section A, or relegated to the Metro section—a matter of only local interest.

The media's analysis deficit combined with its appetite for the negative form a potent one-two punch against schools.

This is not just my jaundiced reading of the situation. U. S. Department of Education staffers Laurence Ogle and Patricia Dabbs also experienced first hand this media foible (1996). It puzzled them. Ogle and Dabbs helped issue the 1996 NAEP geography and history assessments. The geography results were generally positive, wrote Ogle and Dabbs. "The geography press conference was attended by the President of the National Geographic Society and the mood of almost all of the speakers was clearly upbeat . . . The reporting in the press, however, was lackluster and negative, at best. Few agencies picked up the story."

The history release was another matter. The kids didn't do well. The *Washington Post*'s Rene Sanchez called the results dismal. Lewis Lapham of *Harper's* called them a "coroner's report." Reporters beat down the doors to get to Ogle and Dabbs:

> Returning to our offices after the press conference, we found our voice mail jam-packed with media requests for additional information. News accounts were on the radio and reports were even spotted on the Internet [this was 1996, remember, the Net's infancy]. Requests for additional information flooded in from radio and television stations, newspapers, and a few talk-show hosts. . . . Even television's late-night comedy king, Jay Leno, spoke about (and ridiculed) the results. Clearly, the coverage of the negative news eclipsed the relatively good news about geography.

Ogle and Dabbs' experience just reinforced my conclusions expressed two years earlier in an article entitled, "The Media's Myth of School Failure" (Bracey 1994). Naturally, the mainstream media wouldn't publish it. The *Columbia Journalism Review* turned it down on the grounds that, "sadly," the sentiments were too familiar. I came to realize, though, that it wasn't just the media's myth. The media had help. More about that in a moment.

While the media regularly engage in what I call WPSS—Worst Possible Spin Syndrome, the general public manifests what I have deemed The Neurotic Need to Believe the Worst. This is perhaps best seen in the general acceptance of The Lists. I first encountered The Lists on my first day on the job in Cherry Creek Colorado Schools, August 1986. On a bulletin board outside my office was a green sheet of paper containing two lists. The first provided the worst problems in the schools in the 1940s: the second, the same list for the 1980s. The 1940's list contained things like chewing gum, talking out of turn, breaking in line, and so on. The 1980's list was full of violence, gangs, drugs, alcohol, teen pregnancy, and so on.

I recall thinking at the time that I was glad I worked in a school district where those problems didn't dominate. I gave it no more thought. If I had, I would have realized that the list from the 1980s didn't apply to any Colorado district, not even Denver, a district with many of the usual urban problems.

Fortunately, Barry O'Neill at Yale was thinking, "These lists don't look right to me." He decided to track down their origins. In the process, he found the lists widely accepted by people of all political stripes. Among the ideological rainbow of people who had cited them were William J. Bennett, Rush Limbaugh, Phyllis Schlafly, and George Will on the Right, along with Herb Caen, Carl Rowan, and Anna Quindlen. They were variously attributed to CBS news, CQ Researcher, and the Heritage Foundation. They issued, in fact, from a single person, T. Cullen Davis in Forth Worth. Acquitted of murdering his wife's lover, Davis became a born-again Christian. He had taken a hammer to his collection of jade and ivory statues, smashing them as idols of false religion. He had also used his new religious fervor to launch a crusade against the public schools. O'Neill asked Davis how he constructed the list. Davis readily provided his methodology: "How did I know what the offenses in the schools were in 1940? I was there. How do I know what they are now? I read the paper" (O'Neill 1994).

The media also have a proclivity for adopting certain words and phrases that are used over and over again. *Failing schools* is no doubt the most common of these, appearing in dozens, probably hundreds of stories about school reform, privatization, and so on, but always appearing without further explanation, as if no explanation is needed. We all know about them. Another catchword is *dismal* used to describe the performance of failing schools or American students in general, even if to the objective eye the performance looks better. [February 2003: I just conducted an "exact phrase" Google search on *failing schools* and scored 49,700 hits.]

For example, in his story on the PISA results, the *Washington Post's* national education writer, Michael Fletcher, called American kids' scores "dismal." (PISA stands for Program of International Student Assessment, an ongoing project from Paris-based Organization for Economic Cooperation and Development.) In fact, American students scored at slightly above the international average in reading and science and slightly below average in math among the thirty-two nations that participated in the story. This is "dismal?"

The media, left only to their own proclivities, would produce a negative emphasis, but, unfortunately, the media get help from politicians and corporate America. The distortions were particularly rampant during the Reagan and Bush I administrations, but even the Clinton years saw too many of them. As a "liberal," Clinton sought not to destroy public schools but to seek more resources for them. To this end, he took the common tack (common, too, among professors at large research universities) of emphasizing problems. For instance, he more than once said that only 40 percent of American third graders can read independently. Yet, these same third graders had finished second among twenty-seven nations in an international study of reading.

Reagan entered the White House with an education agenda of tuition tax credits, school vouchers, restoring prayer to the schools, and abolishing the U.S. Department of Education. One strategy in putting this agenda in place was to hype the negative and ignore or suppress the positive. The first instance of this was a glorious treasury of selected, spun, and distorted statistics called "A Nation At Risk."

Bell did not want to form a commission or issue a report. As recounted in his memoir, *The Thirteenth Man,* he sought a "Sputnik-like event" that would galvanize Americans into retooling their schools. Unable to find or produce a crisis, he resorted to the commission-and-report route (Bell 1988). "Risk" was, and in some quarters is, hailed as a "landmark" study. In fact, the commissioners selected and spun the statistics, and gave some simplistic interpretations. Some statistics cited might not even exist. When, about a decade after the event, I tried to track down two of them, no one on the commission or on the commission's staff could remember where they came from. The two contended that half of gifted and talented students never match their ability with achievement in school and that college graduates score lower on tests. The document did not say lower on what or than whom, but in any case, we do not test college seniors—the report clearly was not referring to the small minority of seniors who take the GRE.

The most notorious instance of suppression occurred in the case of "The Sandia Report." The Sandia Report, formally known as *Perspectives on Education in America* was a 156-page compilation of data about the condition of public education—dropout rates, high school completion rates, SAT trends, NAEP trends, international comparisons, and so on. Its summary conclusion was, "There are many problems in American education, but there is no system-wide crisis."[2] This was too positive for the Bush administration. When the Sandia engineers came to Washington to present their findings, David Kearns, former Xerox CEO and then Deputy Secretary of Energy, told them, "You bury this or I'll bury you." This I got from one of the engineers. An *Education Week* article account said only, "Administration officials, particularly Mr. Kearns, reacted angrily at the meeting" (Miller 1991).

The report was suppressed. The official reason for nonpublication was that the report was undergoing "peer review," and it is to the eternal shame of Peter House of the National Science Foundation and Emerson Elliott of the U.S. Department of Education that they signed blatantly political critiques of the report. In 2001, I contacted Lee Bray, the first Sandia official to get in touch with me about the report in 1990. Bray had retired several years earlier and didn't want to open old wounds, but he did affirm absolutely that the report was suppressed. It finally saw daylight in 1993 as the entirety of the May/June issue of the *Journal of Educational Research* (Carson, Huelskamp, and Woodall 1993).

More typical of efforts to slant the public's view on education was the very different handling of two international studies. One showed Americans not doing so well in math and science; the other showed Americans almost at the top of the heap in reading. The first appeared in February 1992 (Lapointe, Askew, and Mead 1992; Lapointe, Mead, and Askew 1992). Secretary of Education Lamar Alexander and Assistant Secretary Diane Ravitch orchestrated a large press conference, and the study received wide coverage in both print and electronic media. The study found U.S. students mostly ranked low (although their actual scores were near the international averages). "An 'F' in World Competition" was the headline over *Newsweek*'s story (Kantrowitz and Wingert 1992).

The second study was published five months later in July 1992 (Elley 1992). This time, no press conference occurred. It took *Education Week* over two months to learn of the story and then only by accident. A friend of then-*Education Week* reporter, Robert Rothman, sent him a copy from Europe. *Education Week* gave the study front-page coverage, as did *USA Today*, which played off the *Education Week* story[3] (Rothman 1992; Manning 1992). The *USA Today* story carried a curious quote from Francie Alexander, then a Deputy Assistant Secretary of Education. She dismissed the study as irrelevant to the 1990s.

Why the differential treatment of the two international reports? The math and science study could make U.S. schools look bad, but the reading study could not. U.S. students ranked second among twenty-seven nations as nine-year-olds, and eighth among thirty-one nations as fourteen-year-olds. Only one country, Finland, had a significantly higher score than American fourteen-year-olds. And at both ages, America's best readers outscored even the Finns (although the differences were so small they would not approach statistical significance).

The Bush II administration has acknowledged that poor students are not achieving well, but has put in place a program that will increase, not decrease, the gap—No Child Left Behind. The resources to assist schools are meager, and, indeed, some argue that it will cost twice as much to put the testing requirements in place as the states will receive for implementing it. No doubt this is why at this moment the governor of Vermont has asked for an analysis of what would happen fiscally if the state surrendered its $52 million from the federal government.[4]

One senses, although there is no direct evidence that bears on the subject, that having a former teacher as First Lady has helped mute any would-be school bashers in or around the White House. On the other hand, the education program that Bush first presented to Congress contained plans for the destruction of the public system: provisions for school vouchers. Bush sneaked a provision for tuition tax credits under Congress' radar, and we can expect a return of voucher legislation later—sooner if the Supreme Court rules that the Cleveland voucher program passes First Amendment constitutional muster.[5] Secretary of Education Rod Paige has often referred to "islands of excellence" in the public school system, clearly implying that they are surrounded by seas of mediocrity and failure (see "The No Child Left Behind Act, a Plan for the Destruction of Public Education" in this volume).

> *Politicians and ideologues, teamed with the business community, have helped foster the falsely negative image of education.*

While politicians and ideologues alone have helped foster the falsely negative image of education, they have also teamed with the business community to multiply the impact. Business has long tried to control what is taught in American public schools and how. In 1887, Jane Addams had this to say:

> The business man has, of course, not said to himself, "I will have the public school train office boys and clerks for me, so that I may have them cheap," but he has thought, and sometimes said, "Teach the children to write legibly, to figure accurately and quickly, to acquire habits of punctuality and order; to be prompt to obey and not question why; and you will fit them to make their way in the world as I have made mine" (in Curti 1961, 203)

Similarly, in 1914, William Maxwell, superintendent of schools in New York City, chided business for abandoning its apprentice programs as too expensive and then having the gall to "denounce the public schools as behind the age, as inefficient, as lacking in public spirit" for balking at doing for free what the corporate world had previously paid for (Maxwell 1914, 175–176).

The Addams-Maxwell era was a more polite time than our own, and I am certain that Addams knew very well that the businessman *had often said,* "Train the boys that I may have them cheap." Today, business is mounting a coordinated effort through the National Alliance of Businesses, the Business Roundtable, and their product, Achieve, Inc. IBM CEO Louis V. Gerstner, Jr., has spearheaded the attacks through his "summits," bringing governors and businessmen into collusion. He is hardly alone. Intel CEO Craig Barrett, State Farm CEO Edward Rust, Texas Instruments CEO Thomas Engibus, as well as then-Wisconsin governor Tommy Thompson, and former Secretary of Education William J. Bennett, all took to the op-ed pages of the *New York Times, Washington Post,* and *USA Today* in 2000, 2001, and 2002 to decry the threat that our schools pose to our competitiveness in the global marketplace (Barrett 2001; Engibus and Rust 2000; Bennett 2000; Gerstner 2002; Gerstner and Thompson 2000).

In late 2000, a commission headed by former senator John Glenn released a report claiming we had to improve math and science teaching *Before It's Too Late.* In the body of the text, the clause *before it's too late,* appears not only in italics, but in red ink (National Commission on Mathematics and Science Teaching for the 21st Century 2000). CEOs Barrett and Rust were on the commission. Rust, heading up the Business Roundtable's education taskforce is ubiquitous, giving speeches around the country and writing in a variety of publications, all demeaning the quality of the public schools.

In fact, there is no correlation between achievement, as measured with test scores, and international market competitiveness as defined by the World Economic Forum (WEF). The Forum, a high-powered group in Geneva with close links to economic think tanks at Harvard, ranks seventy-five nations annually on what it calls its Current Competitiveness Index (CCI). Of the seventy-five nations, thirty-eight also had scores on TIMSS. The United States is second on the CCI and 29th on TIMSS math. Korea is second on TIMSS but 27th on competitiveness. And so forth. Overall, the rank-order correlation coefficient between the CCI and TIMSS is .23. And even this overstates the correlation: The bottom seven nations are low on both variables, which contributes to the relationship. If these seven nations are removed, the correlation actually becomes *negative* (although quite small) (Bracey 2002b, 2002c).

The complete TIMSS study has given rise to a new cliché—and distortion. Gerstner used it in his keynote address to the most recent education summit, and Bill Clinton mouthed a version of it. As spoken to the Heritage Foundation by William J. Bennett, the cliché goes like this: "In America today, the longer you stay in school, the dumber you get relative to peers in other industrialized nations" (Bennett 2000).

This statement derives from the fact that American fourthgraders were near the top in TIMSS, American eighth graders were average, and U.S. high school seniors were apparently near the bottom. I contend that the decline from grade 4 to grade 8 is real, though hardly constituting a crisis, but that the decline between grades 8 and 12 is not.

I think the fall off from grades 4 to 8 stems from two sources. First, American textbooks are about three times as thick as in other nations. TIMSS found that American teachers try to cover many more topics than do teachers in other countries. The coverage is by necessity brief and shallow and doesn't "take." Teachers in Europe and Asia spend more time on fewer topics. Second, American educators have traditionally considered the middle school years as the culmination of elementary school, a time for review and consolidation in preparation for high school. Even now, after years of pressure to accelerate mathematics, only about 15 percent of American eighth graders take algebra. About twice that proportion don't even have algebra or pre-algebra as an option.

Other countries have used the middle school years to introduce new material. Thus, Japanese students receive large amounts of algebra in seventh grade and plane geometry in eighth. The scope and sequence of mathematics needs to be rethought, but it is hardly a matter of "getting dumber."

The acceptance of the TIMSS Final Year Study ("Final Year" because, as the TIMSS authors acknowledge, the final year in many countries is not equivalent to the American senior year of high school) requires the uncritical acceptance of a study so methodologically flawed I do not believe I could have gotten it past the undergraduate honors committee at the College of William and Mary, my alma mater. I have analyzed its many flaws elsewhere (Bracey 2000). Suffice to say here that when one compares subgroups of the American cohort who are most like their European peers, one finds American seniors in the middle, the same rank as in eighth grade.

Flawed or no, the TIMSS Final Year Study, as released by the U.S. Department of Education, was raw meat for the press. While the TIMSS Final Year report emphasized the differences in that final year among different nations, the U.S. Department of Education's press conference made it seem that all other nations' final year students were peers with American seniors. That made for a banner day of bad headlines:

> U.S. 12th-graders Rank Poorly in Math and Science, Study Says (Ethan Bronner, *New York Times*)
>
> U.S. High School Seniors Rank Near Bottom (Rene Sanchez, *Washington Post*)
>
> U.S. Seniors Near Bottom in World Test (Debra Viadero, *Education Week*)
>
> Hey! We're #19! (John Leo, *U.S. News & World Report*)
>
> Why America Has the World's Dimmest Bright Kids (Chester E. Finn, Jr., *Wall Street Journal*)

Finn, A former assistant secretary of education, used his *Wall Street Journal* piece to declare that the TIMSS study proved that American education was "an ossified government bureaucracy incapable of reforming itself" (Finn 1998).

It's too bad the TIMSS data weren't released a couple of months later, after John Schwartz of the *Washington Post* had written "Pat Journalism: When We Prepackage the News, We Miss the Story" (Schwartz 1998). Schwartz usually covers science, but because the reporters who would have normally covered the Jonesboro killings were all on assignment, editors assigned Schwartz to the job. Watching other reporters in Jonesboro, Schwartz observed that "journalists looking for quick answers out of Jonesboro seemed to have brought them along in their luggage." When Schwartz examined the "pat journalism" explanations for the killings, they all fell apart. Even when reporters wrote insightful stories, they were stymied by editors back home who wanted the stories to emphasize "young white crackers shooting each other."

With a stretch, almost any societal failing can be placed at the feet of or on the backs of the schools. An email I received from Abigail Thernstrom, co-author of *America in Black and White,* argued that the unthinking reporters and editors described by Schwartz were themselves evidence that our schools have failed.

I have not yet seen the finger pointed at schools for the Enron, Arthur Andersen, and Global Crossing fiascoes, but watch for it once the trials get started.

Can we expect better coverage in the future? Hard to say. As this is written, it is only May 2002, and I've already had two op-eds in the *Washington Post* (Bracey 2002a, 2002b). On the other hand, a *Post* article on Edison schools looked like a plant to help its sinking stock price (Mathews 2002). Mathews advised he was writing under extreme time duress and the piece was not up to his usual level. One wonders where the impetus came from. It seems unlikely that the media, corporate executives, free market ideologues, and politicians can easily give up such a handy scapegoat.[6]

It is now Spring 2003. I've had one more *Post* article, but none in *USA Today* or the *New York Times*. Articles that I thought decent have been turned down by *The Nation*, *Mother Jones*, the *New Yorker*, the *Atlantic Monthly*, and the *American Prospect*. "Those Misleading SAT and NAEP Trends," Chapter 16, I tried releasing as news, not as an essay under my name. Only one reporter, Gregg Toppo of *USA Today*, showed interest. And he got back to me to say he couldn't interest his editor because the story didn't have a good link to a newsy event.

Notes

1. When Rothstein's editor retired, Rothstein was dismissed in the Fall of 2002. The *Times* still publishes an article on education each Wednesday, now written by staff education writer Michael Winerip.

2. This statement did not appear in the published version.

3. The *USA Today* story carries a publication date one day earlier than the *Education Week* story, but *Education Week* often arrives in mailboxes two days before the official publication date.

4. Since this was written, Vermont has apparently capitulated, perhaps because the governor wants to be president. It will keep the testing program it has in place, but add a separate one to satisfy federal mandates. It will do this despite an analysis indicating that it will receive $52 million from the federal government, but spend $158 million implementing the new program.

5. The Supreme Court ruled the vouchers were constitutional. Several states have introduced voucher legislation, and Bush has put $76 million into his fiscal 2004 budget for a voucher program in Washington, D.C.

6. It is now March, 2003. Education has largely disappeared from the media, displaced by the laments over the Bush budget and tax plan, the sinking economy, the war with Iraq, and the ignoring of the crisis with North Korea. A few stories have mentioned the rising tide of disillusionment with No Child Left Behind, but the *Washington Post* and, wholly predictably, the *Wall Street Journal* have editorially supported Bush's voucher plans for the District.

References

Barrett, Craig. 2001. Interview with editors of *USA Today*. Printed in the November 8, 2001 edition.

Bell, Terrell H. 1988. *The Thirteenth Man: A Reagan Cabinet Memoir.* New York: Free Press.

Bennett, William J. 2000. "The State, and Future of American Education." Speech to the Heritage Foundation, March. Accessible at www.heritage.org

Bracey, Gerald W. 2002a. "What They Did on Vacation: It's Not Schools That Are Failing Poor Kids." *Washington Post*, January 16, p. A19.

———. 2002b. "Why Do We Scapegoat the Schools?" *Washington Post*, May 5, p. B1.

———. 2002c. "Test Scores, Creativity, and Global Competitiveness." *Phi Delta Kappan*, June.

———. 2000. "The TIMSS 'Final Year' Study and Report: A Critique." *Educational Researcher*, May, pp. 4–10.

———. 1997. *The TRUTH About America's Schools: The Bracey Reports 1991–1997.* Bloomington, IN: Phi Delta Kappa International.

———. 1994. "The Media's Myth of School Failure." *Education Leadership*, September, pp. 80–84.

Carson, C. C., R. M. Huelskamp, and T. D Woodall. 1993. "Perspectives on Education in America: An Annotated Briefing." *Journal of Educational Research*, May/June, pp. 259–310.

Curti, Merle. 1961. *The Social Ideas of American Educators*. Patterson, NJ: Littlefield, Adams.

Elley, Warwick P. 1992. *How in the World Do Students Read?* Hamburg: Grindledruck. Available in the United States through the International Reading Association, Dover, Delaware.

Engibus, Thomas J., and Edward B. Rust. 2000. "The Nation's 'Help Wanted' Crisis. *Washington Post,* September 7, p. A25.

Finn, Chester E., Jr. 1998. "Why the United States Has the World's Dimmest Bright Students." *Wall Street Journal,* February 25, p. A22.

Gerstner, Louis V., Jr. 2002. "The Tests We Know We Need." *New York Times,* March 14, p. A31.

Gerstner, Louis V. Jr., and Tommy G. Thompson. 2000. "The Problem Isn't the Kids." *New York Times,* December 8, p. A39.

Harwood, Richard. 1994. "Reporting On, By and For an Elite." *Washington Post,* May 28, p. A21.

Henry, Tamara. 2001. "Scores Go Up for Charters." *USA Today,* March 28, p. D9.

Kantrowitz, Barbara, and Pat Wingert. 1992. "An 'F' in World Competition." *Newsweek,* February 17, p. 57.

Lapointe, Archie E., Janet M. Askew, and Nancy A. Mead. 1992. *Learning Mathematics.* Princeton, NJ: Educational Testing Service.

Lapointe, Archie E., Nancy A. Mead, and Janet M. Askew. 1992. *Learning Science.* Princeton, NJ: Educational Testing Service.

Manning, Anita. 1992. "U. S. Kids Near Top of Class in Reading." *USA Today,* September 29, p. A1. (Note: Although the *USA Today* article is dated before Robert Rothman's article on the same topic in *Education Week, Education Week* often arrives in mailboxes two days before its official publication date.)

Mathews, Jay. 2002. "Putting For-Profit Company to the Test." *Washington Post,* April 30, p. A9.

Maxwell, William. 1914. "On a Certain Arrogance in Educational Theorists." *Educational Review*, February, pp. 175–76.

Miller, Julie. 1991. "Report Questioning 'Crisis' in Education Triggers an Uproar." *Education Week,* October 9, p. 1.

National Commission on Mathematics and Science Teaching for the 21st Century. 2000. *Before It's Too Late.* Washington, DC: U.S. Department of Education.

Ogle, Laurance, and Patricia Dabbs. 1996. "Good News Bad News: Does Media Coverage of Schools Promote Scattershot Remedies?" *Education Week,* March 13, p. 46

O'Neill, Barry. 1994. "Anatomy of a Hoax. *New York Times Sunday Magazine,* March 6, pp. 46–49.

Oplinger, Doug and Dennis J. Willard. 2002. "Business Breaks Costing Schools." *Akron Beacon Journal,* April 10, p. A1.

Oplinger, Doug, and Dennis J. Willard. 1999a. "In Education, Money Talks." *Akron Beacon Journal,* December 13, p. A1.

———. 1999b. "Voucher System Falls Far Short of Goals." *Akron Beacon Journal,* December 14, p. A1.

———. 1999c. "Campaign Organizer Pushes Hard for Changes." *Akron Beacon Journal,* December 15, p. A1.

Reaves, Joseph. 2002. *Falling in Line: An Examination of Education Editorials Appearing in Four Leading U.S. Newspapers from the Inauguration of George W. Bush to September 11, 2001.* Available at www.asu.edu.edu/educ/epsl/epru.htm (Click on "Archives Research Reports.")

Rothman, Robert. 1992. "U.S. Ranks High in International Study of Reading Achievement," *Education Weekly,* September 30, p. 1.

Schwartz, John. 1998. "Pat Journalism: When We Prepackage the News, We Miss the Story." *Washington Post,* April 19, 1998, p. C1.

Willard, Dennis J., and Doug Oplinger. 1999a. "Charter Experiment Goes Awry: Schools Fail to Deliver." *Akron Beacon Journal,* December 12, p. A1.

———. 1999b. "Voucher Plan Leaves Long List of Broken Vows." *Akron Beacon Journal,* December 14, p. A1.

———. 1999c. "School Battle Eludes Voters, Takes Its Cues from Coalitions." *Akron Beacon Journal,* December 15, p. A1.

The Right's Data-Proof Ideologues

ost of my colleagues and I work in some sector of educational
research. We researchers deal with data. We try to be disinterested with regard to what the data say, letting them guide us
wherever possible. This neutralist stance puts us at quite a disadvantage when dealing with people whose ideologies make them data-
proof. This weakness is now of great importance because we're up
against a group of ideologically driven, Right-wing public school
critics with an agenda for changing, perhaps eliminating, American
public schools. Their ideologies act as prisms, blocking or at best
distorting what the data on American education actually say.

They are at war with the rest of those in education. Jerry
Falwell and Pat Robertson have both issued declarations of war
against the larger society. "This is an intellectual, conceptual, and
ideological war," the Hudson Institute's Chester E. Finn, Jr., said
in the August 24, 1994, *Washington Times*. Because this exact
quote also appears in a Hudson Institute publication, we may
safely assume it is not a misattribution. The *Times* article also
declared that the Hudson Institute was gearing up for war and
called Mr. Finn a "bomb thrower," apparently with approbation.
Bomb throwers, in any case, are not generally thought to be seeking facts that contradict their beliefs.

I first noticed the Right's data-proof stance when I debated Diane Ravitch, then Assistant U.S. Secretary of Education, at the 1992 Education Writers Association meeting. We were given the question "Are American schools as bad as they say?" I had recently published a long article, with mountains of data that compelled the answer "no." I spoke first and presented as many facts as I could in the twenty minutes allotted. Ms. Ravitch then began her "side" of the "debate" with, "That's not really an interesting question," and proceeded to deliver a digressive discourse on the history of American education. The back and forth that followed the opening statements was no more satisfying.

A short time later, I debated Denis Doyle, then a senior fellow at the Hudson Institute, on the same question. At one point, Mr. Doyle said that "expenditures for schools increased in the 1980s by 34 percent, in real dollars, but test scores were static." I quickly dug into my collection of overheads, threw onto the screen two slides showing that test scores at all grades 3 to 12 had been rising since the mid-70s. At all grades save grade 8 and grade 12, scores were at all-time highs, and those two grades approached record levels.

Mr. Doyle regarded the curves and said, "Well, the important ones, the SATs, are static." I acknowledged that the overall average of the SATs has been flat for a while, largely because the composition of SAT takers had been changing. The standards on what is now called the Scholastic Assessment Test were set on 10,654 students living in the Northeast. Ninety-eight percent of them were white, 60 percent of them were male, and 40 percent of them had received their high school educations in private schools. Currently, those who take the SAT are 31 percent minority and 52 percent women, and 30 percent of them report annual family incomes under $30,000. All of these changes are associated with lower test scores. If one takes these demographic changes into account, SAT scores have been rising also.

I figured this irrefutable test-score information would eventually sink into Mr. Doyle and that would be the end of it. Hardly. In 1994, a book, *Reinventing Education,* appeared. Of the four authors, Louis V. Gerstner, Jr., the chief executive officer of the International Business Machines Corporation, was listed first and Mr. Doyle third, although many of the passages were simple extracts from recent articles and speeches by Mr. Doyle. Their

book propagated many inaccuracies, but I was especially surprised by a sentence on page 229: "Expenditures for public education increased in the decade of the 1980s by 34 percent (in real
dollars), yet the only output measures available were test scores,
which were, by and large, static." Not only had the facts not been
absorbed, but the statement was also presented with virtually the
same syntax as it had been two years earlier.

Reinventing Education also propounded another favorite assertion of the education Right: The United States spends more
money on public schools than any other nation in the world. A
mantra during George H. W. Bush's
years, it is still popular. The well-
known policy analyst and conservative
school critic Herbert Walberg, of the
University of Illinois at Chicago,
recently made this claim. When I cited
him in print and said it wasn't so, Mr.
Walberg rushed a letter to the editor in
his defense. He referred to the U.S.
Education Department's *Condition of
Education* as validating his contention. Sure enough, one chart in
the 1992 edition does show the United States spending most. The
figure is in terms of dollars spent, a computation that takes no
account of rate fluctuations or purchasing power. Much more
importantly, the chart shows the United States and only five other
nations. It is astonishing that Mr. Walberg, a man of long experience in the analysis of international data, is willing to define the
world, and the United States rank in it, using only six countries.

> *To "prove" that the United
> States spends more money
> on schools than any other
> nation, researcher Herbert
> J. Walberg referred to a
> chart that only included
> seven countries.*

If one moves to a longer list, as the *Condition of Education* has
done in its 1994 edition, the United States loses its number-one
rank very quickly. There are various ways of calculating school
expenditures, and there are problems with all of them in terms of
their comparability across countries. Taking Mr. Walberg's preferred measure, dollars spent per year, for the nineteen nations of
the Organization for Economic Cooperation and Development
(OECD), the United States finishes sixth. Thus, even using Mr.
Walberg's chosen index, the figures do not bear him out.

Other ways of calculating costs involve expenditures as a percent of gross domestic product or of per-capita gross domestic
product. The first does not take into account the size of the GDP;

the second does. In both, the United States attains only an average, tenth place, ranking among the nineteen OECD nations. And even this ranking is misleading, because in this country, fewer of the dollars make it into the classroom. U.S. schools provide many services not provided in other nations, or provided to a lesser degree: transportation, food, medical services, counseling, and, especially, special education. Because of these extra services, the United States is the only nation in which teachers constitute fewer than half of schools' employees.

To these comments, the conservative critics would no doubt respond, "It doesn't matter if we're number one in spending or not; it doesn't help to throw money at the problem. Money is not related to achievement." Indeed, that is precisely what the University of Rochester economist Eric Hanushek and Mr. Finn said at a recent Brookings Institution symposium. They reiterated the claim that we're spending more money, but test scores are flat. When I held up a chart showing test scores at even higher levels than when I debated Mr. Doyle two years earlier, they appeared unconcerned and unimpressed. It's because they have no intention of letting facts alter their opinions.

Those who allege that money is unrelated to achievement are fond of citing Mr. Hanushek's analysis. Yet, at least two more sophisticated analyses of his data clearly find that they do not support Mr. Hanushek's contentions. Other recent, more empirical research by Ronald Ferguson of Harvard University, Howard Wainer of the Educational Testing Service, and Robert Lockwood of the Alabama Department of Education and James McLean of the University of Alabama plainly shows that money does matter.

> To "prove" that money is unrelated to achievement, Bennett, Novak, and Will all ignored the fact that in very high scoring states, few students take the SAT.

When not ignoring data, the ideologues use them deceitfully. In 1993, the conservative American Legislative Exchange Council released yet another study demeaning the potency of money in educational attainment. In this study, directed by former U.S. Secretary of Education William J. Bennett, the annual per-pupil cost at the state level defined expenditures, and state-level SAT scores defined achievement. A comrade-in-doctrinaireness, the syndicated columnist George Will, looked at Mr. Bennett's report and penned a column, "Meaningless Money Factor." Mr. Will observed that the states with the highest SAT scores—Iowa, North Dakota, South Dakota, Utah, and Minnesota—all were low spenders. New Jersey, on the other hand, spent more money per child per year than anyone else and still finished only 39th in the great SAT race. A few days later, the columnist and talk-show host Robert Novak tried to terrify the good citizens of California by revealing that California's SAT average was lower than Mississippi's.

> *Those who allege that money is unrelated to achievement are fond of citing Mr. Hanushek's analysis.*

In addition to ignoring differences in purchasing power in the different states, what Messrs. Bennett, Will, and Novak failed to point out was that in the high-scoring states, no one takes the SAT. For the top five states, the percentages of seniors who bubbled in SAT answer sheets the year of the study were 5, 6, 6, 4, and 10, respectively. In New Jersey, on the other hand, 76 percent of the senior class huddled in angst on Saturday mornings. In a similar situation, Mississippi beat California because 4 percent of its seniors took the SAT while 47 percent of California's did. One might wish to applaud New Jersey for encouraging three-fourths of its students to apply to four-year institutions that require the SAT.

Along with the claims that we spend more money than anyone and that money doesn't matter, Messrs. Hanushek, Finn, Doyle, and Gerstner have also accused American students of looking awful in international comparisons. They can say this only because they don't bother to look at the data. If they looked at the data, they'd be rendered mute.

For instance, in a 1992 international study of reading skills in thirty-one nations, which was almost entirely ignored by the media, American nine-year-olds finished second only to Finland. That's right, those TV-drenched couch potatoes finished second only to a small, homogeneous country that spends few hours worrying about how to teach Finnish as a second language. American fourteen-year-olds finished eighth, still in the upper third, but the scores of all the high-ranked countries were clumped so close that, again, only Finland had significantly higher scores.

This last finding, tightly bunched scores among most nations, points to another subtlety that conservatives like to ignore. They prefer to deal in ranks, but ranks obscure performance. In the Second International Assessment of Educational Progress (the IAEP-2), American nine-year-olds finished third in the world in science among fifteen nations. Our fourteen-year-olds didn't rank so well: thirteenth of fifteen. But both groups had scores very close to average. If the fourteen-year-olds had mustered only 5 percent more of the items correct, they'd have finished fifth. If the nine-year-olds had failed 5 percent more, they'd have been near the bottom. The differences among most countries in these international comparisons are so small that they have no educational or policy uses—only political and ideological ones.

Even in mathematics, where we are such putative dolts, our students perform much better than people claim. "Last or next to last," said Mr. Gerstner and company. "Dead last," said the *Washington Post* pundit Charles Krauthammer. Wrong again, guys. In the Second International Mathematics Study (SIMS) and the IAEP-2, the scores were mostly close to average.

But looking at the average of all American students is misleading (even when we do well). In SIMS, Japanese students had the highest average scores, but the top 20 percent of American students outscored the top 20 percent of Japanese students, and the top 50 percent of American classes had a score identical to that of the top 50 percent of Japanese classes. In the IAEP-2, Korea and Taiwan had the highest averages, but Asian students in American schools scored higher and white students tied Hungary for third place. Black and Hispanic students, though, and students in disadvantaged urban areas, scored below the lowest country, Jordan, or state, Mississippi.

Why do the conservatives insist on ignoring all the complexities of the data? There are several reasons. One is that they simply do not like to deal with complexities, because complexities are messy. More than liberals, conservatives are guilty of what Harold Howe II calls "millennialist thinking," thinking that a single social reform can bring the millennium. The conservatives' search for fine-sounding, simple solutions brings to mind H. L. Mencken's comment, "For every complex problem there is a simple answer—and it's wrong."

> *Why do the conservatives insist on ignoring all the complexities of the data? One reason: They do not like to deal with complexities.*

In addition to an affinity for simplistic solutions, the conservatives display a breathtaking rigidity and narrowness of thought. The educational leadership fraternity, Phi Delta Kappa, and a liberal Washington think tank, the Institute for Educational Leadership, tried to organize a conference called "Common Ground." The goal was to bring liberal and conservative education thinkers together and determine where they could agree. The Hudson Institute was asked to cosponsor the event and initially declined. Finally, after a foundation put up the funds, the conservatives agreed to show up, but it was clear that they felt they had nothing to learn, nothing in common with the liberals. When one attendee mentioned the polls that find people approve of their local schools, Hudson's Mr. Doyle commented, "That's just scientific proof that ignorance is bliss."

And, finally, while liberals often offer a diverse range of options for educational reform, and don't always agree with each other, conservatives present a narrow platform they've agreed on and they talk only to each other. The "Education Policy Committee," recently formed by Mr. Finn and Ms. Ravitch as part of the Hudson Institute's Educational Excellence Network, contains virtually no one in its list of forty-five members whose views would do anything but reinforce the narrow conceits of the political Right. Those few who could broaden the discourse were identified with asterisks next to their names as not agreeing with the committee's first report. And in these narrow conceits, they have decided they can and should overlook those aspects of the data that might prove them wrong. The consequence is that they have perpetrated nasty disinformation about the condition of American schools, for which they should be ashamed—but, no doubt, aren't.

Horace Mann and Today's Mandates
A Talk to the Horace Mann League

I am deeply honored and moved to receive this award, especially when I think of the many who could easily be so honored.
I only wish I could accept it in a happier time. I am haunted these days by photos of the American and Northern Alliance entry into Kabul, showing Afghanis celebrating their arrival as the Parisians did nearly sixty years earlier.

Then I imagine a photo in which a group of teachers and administrators arrive at a school in an armored personnel carrier to liberate it and are greeted by the cheering teachers and children incarcerated in the building as they throw off the burqaa of high-stakes testing.

I am not sanguine that we will see this anytime soon, because from what I hear, when the rules and regs governing the new elementary and secondary education act are revealed, we will discover that the Taliban have fled Kandahar only to take up residence on Maryland Avenue in the nation's capital.[1]

I can only hope that there are teachers abroad in the land who are following the lead of Afghani artists. Under the Taliban, these artists contin-

> *I hope that teachers across the country are sneaking in creativity and inspiration underneath the state mandates.*

ued to paint what their consciences and talents dictated, but then painted over their authentic works with images that the Taliban censors would approve. I hope that teachers across the country are sneaking in creativity and inspiration underneath the state mandates.

Whenever a system is imposed on people from without and without their approval, people will attempt to game the system.

Thus, we find teachers instructed to concentrate on children whose scores are near the passing score or, as in California, children whose gains will improve the schools rankings in the affluent parents index, something they officially call the Academic Progress Index (API) in Sacramento. All test scores are highly correlated with socioeconomic status, but I have never seen such enormous correlations as between California's API and indices of economic well-being, one reason many people in California refer to the API as the "affluent parents index." It's a measure of the number of Lexuses per acre.

In states that are concentrating on reading and math, we find other subjects, not only art, physical education, and recess, but also science and social studies, disappearing from the school day. A few years ago, by the way, Richard Rothstein, predicting such distorted emphases when the criteria for accountability were narrowly construed, elaborated an accountability system for Los Angeles that went a long way to providing balance and coherence.[2]

One might excuse these excesses if our educational system were desperate, but by and large it is not. At least, not for the majority of American students.

Consider these numbers second, seventh, and fourth. Those are the ranks of white American fifteen-year-olds in reading, mathematics, and science, respectively, in the recent PISA (Program of International Student Assessment) study from OECD. Thirty-two countries participated, mostly wealthy European nations.

It is now obvious that the standards movement is increasing, not decreasing, the gap, because resources have not flowed into the schools that need them.

Now consider these numbers: twenty-ninth, thirtieth, and thirtieth. These are the ranks for both black and Hispanic students.

It is obvious that we have a problem here. It is also now obvious that the standards movement is *increasing,* not decreasing, the gap, because resources have not flowed into economically impoverished schools to permit them to cope with the new, sometimes draconian, standards and tests.

As educators attempt to cope with mandates, we see scenes that are not pretty, scenes that reflect despotism, not democracy. We find school people doing things that they should not do.

We find Birmingham, Alabama, expelling 522 low-scoring students just before administering the state tests and then firing the teacher who brought that act to public attention.[3]

We find Gwinnett County, Georgia, sending school policemen—policemen, not security guards—all the way to Vermont to threaten an educator with a felony charge because she received a copy of the Gwinnett County test, which, I can tell you authoritatively, is a scam. Gwinnett authorities also fired and suspended for life the teaching credentials of a teacher who put six test items up on a website to show parents what was on the test.[4]

We find the state of Colorado setting its "proficient" level at the equivalent of the 90th percentile on a norm-referenced test in mathematics, and its "advanced level" at the 99th percentile.

We find the state of Virginia setting similarly outrageously high passing scores on its twenty-one state-mandated tests.

We find the state of Massachusetts threatening to withdraw funds from a conference if anti-tester Alfie Kohn is not disinvited to speak. Kohn did not speak but got paid anyway. Happily, the Massachusetts ACLU has filed suit on Kohn's behalf.[5]

We find a teacher in Chicago considering the city's tests so awful that he published them in his monthly newspaper. Chicago fired the teacher and sued him for $1.4 million, the cost, it claimed of replacing items that never should have been used in the first place.[6] Some of the questions had no right answer, some of them had multiple right answers, and some of them presented factually incorrect history.

What would Horace Mann think of all this?

I think he would champion the idea of state-level standards, although he would recoil at some of the draconian sanctions that have accompanied their imposition. Still, Mann fought for a centralized state system and a core curriculum. Various people tried to abolish Mann's state board of education and to return all education oversight to localities. Mann thought this a mistake. As a state legislator, Mann looked around at all of the adult depravity and debauchery that characterized Boston in the second quarter of the 19th century and resolved to save the next generation. (He believed in the perfectibility of man.) He would save it neither through religion nor through the family. He would do it through education, and he wanted it available to all. He thought he needed a state-directed system to accomplish this.

At the same time, Mann rejected another model of education that was being touted by some as the appropriate model for America: the Prussian system. In a tour of German schools that was brief and, no doubt, highly orchestrated by his hosts to show off the best, Mann was impressed by the teachers' training and by their pedagogy. But he found the Prussian system far too coercive and authoritarian in nature, and abhorred the central tenet of that system: absolute loyalty and obedience to the state.

What we have seen in various states, and what we will see coming out from the U.S. Department of Education looks more like an authoritarian system than a democratic one. I think Mann would be appalled.

Mann, after all, and maybe *above* all, wanted to make education more humane. Some of his goals were practical and concrete and things we would take for granted today. For instance, Mann wanted to get rid of corporal punishment and to give each child a chair, not the curvature-inducing backless benches that were then in use.

> *If you teach people right, Mann believed, they will love to learn.*

More importantly, Mann focused on character and learning. Although he never, to my knowledge, used the phrase "lifelong learning," that is what he sought. If you teach people right, he believed, they will love to learn.

Again, I thank you for this honor and I can only hope that we can return soon to the kind of humane, democratic system that Horace Mann envisioned.

Notes

1. Alas, this has proved true. See Chapter 1, "The No Child Left Behind Act." Maryland Avenue is the location of the U.S. Department of Education.

2. Rothstein, at the time an education columnist for the *New York Times,* received the "Outstanding Friend of Education" at the same meeting. His accountability system was never used.

3. The teacher started his own school to help these children.

4. Courts later reversed these actions.

5. The suit is in progress, but as of Spring 2003, there has been no resolution.

6. In a settlement, the ludicrous $1.4 million was dropped to $500.

The End of Childhood

I'm a slow learner, but I realized that this high-standards, high-stakes testing thing in schools had gone too far when I read that the Virginia Beach, Virginia, school board convened a special meeting to decide if it should mandate recess in the district's elementary schools. So many of its teachers and principals were so uptight about passing the state tests, that many of them had abandoned the kids' play time. Imagine, having to legislate recess. Some schools have kicked out art, music, and physical education; museum trips; and whale watching: "Whale watching is not on the test," said a superintendent, explaining why the annual trip had been canceled.

Imagine having to legislate recess.

Childhood has been canceled, too. I should have seen it coming. Around 1995, the cartoon strip, "Sally Forth," predicted it clearly. The strip began with daughter Hilary saying she might need help with her geography project.

"What's your project?" asks Sally.
"We get two choices. The first is to build a working model of the Panama Canal."
"What's the second, make a relief map of the Andes?"

"How did you know?"

At this point, husband Ted pipes up with, "Whatever happened to the good old days? My fourth grade geography project was to list North Carolina's natural resources."

So was mine, except it was Virginia. Later came Assyria's natural resources list, then China's. No more. I thought the strip funny at the time; now I realize it was an omen. Here is a tenth grade social studies objective from the Virginia Standards of Learning Program:

> The student will analyze the regional development of Asia, Africa, the Middle East, Latin America, and the Caribbean in terms of physical, economic, and cultural characteristics and historical evolution from 1000 A.D. to the present.

Gee, they left out Australia and New Zealand.

Researchers at the Mid Continent Educational Research Laboratory looked around at all of the standards brought forth by professional organizations such as the National Council of Teachers of Mathematics, and asked, "How long would it take for students to learn all of them?" Their answer? About the same amount of time required to get a Ph.D. The researchers' conclusion, in all seriousness, was that the *brightest* students could get through the standards by age twenty-seven.

The researchers' conclusion, in all seriousness, was that the brightest students could get through the standards by age twenty-seven.

The high-standards, high-stakes movement has given us new ways of measuring educational excellence: How many students are throwing up on test day, how many children are taking Prozac, and how much do their textbook-laden backpacks weigh? The *Florida Times Union* actually went out and measured the weight kids carry on their backs. Some *elementary* schools had children walking around with nineteen pounds on their shoulders. The *Philadelphia Inquirer* reported that some high school kids, carrying twenty-four to twenty-eight pounds, hunched over like peasants in Third World countries. It also reported orthopedists saying that their bodies suffer the consequences: muscle fatigue, scoliosis, and spondylitis (a spinal inflammation).

Remember kindergarten? It's a German word. It means, or meant, "children's garden." Not any more. Recently I was waiting in a foyer with another person for clearance into a military building. My wait-companion asked what I was doing there. I said speaking on the condition of public education and the current tough standards. I had pushed a button. She launched into a diatribe about the godawful amount of homework her kindergartner brings home every night. A friend in Washington State says he has to read a book a day to his kindergartner, and has to sign a form to prove it. Whatever happened to play?

Why are we doing this to our children? Well, we *say* it's in the name of high standards, although clearly, in some states, one goal has been to make the public schools look bad in order to grease the skids for vouchers. So why are we pressing draconian standards on the children? What is the terrible state of society that requires them?

Look, the Cold War is over. We won, and now we send American astronauts to repair the Russian-built part of the International Space Station. It's impossible to get from the new war on terrorism to the need for higher standards. The logic doesn't work. When the Soviet Union was the enemy and space technology and rocketry were key, the argument for more and better engineers had some surface validity, but you can't make that argument when the enemy's principal modus operandi is to blow you up, usually along with himself. Shall we now teach bomb-building in shop, and germ warfare in biology?

The economy is in a shambles but, thank heaven, economists look to Bush's tax-cut-and-spend-anyway policies. In earlier times, responsibility for recessions was laid at the schoolhouse door. When the 1990–1992 recession hit, many blamed the schools for a loss of competitiveness. In 1983, "A Nation At Risk" had tightly linked high test scores to economic well-being, and our kids looked middling in international comparisons. But then the economy soared (too fast! too high! said Alan Greenspan; no credit to the schools for the recovery, said the critics) while Europe stagnated, Japan lolled in apparently terminal recession, and those "Asian Tiger" economies tanked.

Even on international comparisons, our kids on the whole are doing much better than critics think. Oh, I concede immediately that city schools and poor rural schools both need a lot of help.

But consider these numbers:

1. Standardized test scores are at record levels. Scores declined from about 1965 to about 1975 (a decade of substantial social unrest, turmoil, and war that many people remember only in flashbacks), then climbed to all-time highs.[1]

2. The proportion of students scoring above 650 on the SAT math test is at an all-time high, something that cannot be attributed to the "math gene" of Asian students. The proportion grew by 90 percent from 1981 to 2001; with Asian kids taken out of the sample, the growth was still 67 percent.

3. Scores on the National Assessment of Educational Progress (NAEP) have shown substantial gains in reading, math, and science, especially when examined separately for each ethnicity. This is the appropriate analysis, because when NAEP began, minorities were a much smaller proportion of the total sample than now. Even looking at scores with all ethnic groups combined, though, the trends show that all three subject areas are at record highs at all three ages tested. (For a description of the "appropriate analysis," see "Those Misleading SAT and NAEP Trends," in this volume.)

4. The number of students taking advanced placement examinations has risen from 2,000 in 1956 to 78,000 in 1978 to 704,000 in 1999 to 937,951 in 2002. In 2002, those 937,951 students sat for 1,585,516 tests.

5. In 1982, 14 percent of high school graduates had earned four credits in English and three each in social studies, math, and science. In 1994, before the current standards movement ran amok, it had already risen to 50 percent and it continues to rise.

6. In a 1992 international comparison of reading skills, American students were second. Our 90th, 95th, and 99th percentiles were higher than any of the thirty other countries in the study. That is, our best readers scored higher than any other nation's best readers. In a 2003 comparison, only three of thirty-two nations had significantly higher scores.

Perhaps the best microcosmic data (representing the whole in a small set of figures), come from PISA (Program of International

Student Assessment), released by the Organization for Economic Cooperation and Development (OECD) in December 2001. OECD tested fifteen-year-olds in thirty-two nations in reading, math, and science. Overall, American students ranked slightly above average in reading and science and slightly below average in math. The U.S. Department of Education released scores by ethnicity. There were no ranks for Asian Americans because in a study such as PISA, they form too small a sample to provide a reliable estimate for the whole group. But here are the ranks for the three largest ethnic groups in the United States:

	Reading	Math	Science
White students	2nd	7th	4th
Black students	29th	30th	30th
Hispanic students	29th	30th	30th

When you consider that about half of black and Hispanic students live in poverty and consider further that poverty has a huge impact on learning, it becomes clear where resources are needed. We don't need a program that tests all children every year in reading, math, and science in grades 3 through 8 to know where the problems are.

Historians have contended that the concept of childhood as a special time evolved over about three centuries. Three centuries ago, that concept did not exist. Societies considered children as miniature adults and treated them accordingly: no special clothes, no special games. Children were widely regarded as carrying some innate depravity that had to be beaten out of them, but otherwise they were just little people.

The standards movement, alas, has returned to the conception that children are just small grownups, and the consequences could be severe.

Twentieth-century theoreticians such as Jean Piaget showed that children don't think as adults (at age 4, my grandson asked his mother why my wife and I had no children like him and his sister). The standards movement, alas, has returned to the conception that children are just small grownups, and the consequences could be severe. Throwing up on test day could be the least of it.

When I was a kid, adults often counseled me to enjoy what

they knowingly said were the best years of my life. What adult would dare tell that to a child panicked over possibly repeating third grade because of a low test score? And who among our children having such dreadful experiences in school would then ever want to consider a career as a . . . teacher?

Note

1. Since this was first written in 2000, scores for the best source of test-trend data, the "Iowas" have dropped a little. It is not clear why. At first, the developers of the Iowas thought it might be too much emphasis on self-esteem. Then they conjectured that it might be that the high-standards movement was actually backfiring. More recently, they've come to my position: It's probably demographics. We continue to receive many immigrants, most of whom share one common quality: They don't speak English as a native language.

24 The Testing–Talent Disconnect

> With all, it was now clear that among, say, eight
> kids reading at between 4.5 and 4.8 grade level,
> there were in fact eight kids, some of whom
> were reading all kinds of stuff, some who would
> only read the newspaper, some who would only
> read *Mad* magazine—or look at it anyway—and
> some who wouldn't read anything at all. Thus
> the test could only mean something if you never
> looked at the kids themselves.
>
> James Herndon, *How to Survive
> in Your Native Land*, 1971

Late in the Friday afternoon of my first week as a school district
testing director, a distraught parent called. "I can't make it
through the weekend without talking to *someone*," she moaned.
She had just received her son's standardized test scores. Her son
had scored below 90 percent of the kids in the country.

"We've been raising Paul on the assumption that he would
go to college. The *teachers* have all thought he was a nice and
intelligent boy. Do we have to *completely* arrange our expectations for what Paul can do?" Some 85 percent of this district's
kids would head out to four-year colleges, so the mother's concern was not obsessive or pushy. I felt, though, it was a little
early to foreclose on Paul's academic future. Paul was nine
years old.

At the moment, however, the tests
told this mother that her kid was no
damn good at things academic, and
they told her Paul's teachers were
wrong. Worse, the test scores told her
that Paul *ought* to be doing better. The

> *The tests told his mother
> that her kid was no damn
> good at things academic,
> and they told her Paul's
> teachers were wrong.*

testing company used ability test scores to make predictions about achievement test scores. According to Paul's ability tests, he ought to be scoring above 75 percent of all kids, not below 90 percent.

Had she talked with Paul's teachers, I inquired. No, they weren't back from summer vacation yet. The principal? Yes, but he said this was the first time these tests had been used, and he wouldn't talk to her until he had talked to me. I silently cursed the principal for ducking. I told her to call Pupil Services, and I would try to reach the principal.

I pulled Paul's records and answer sheets. I noticed that on the verbal section of the ability test, he had answered fewer than half the questions, but all of those he did try were right. The quantitative ability section showed no patterns, but its instructions were pretty complicated, and if Paul were having trouble with *words*, he might easily have had trouble understanding what he was supposed to do.

The third part of the ability test is called "nonverbal." It's perceptually oriented. An item might start with a series of geometric figures and ask the student which of five other figures would be the next one in the series. On this part of the test, Paul had outscored 91 percent of all other third graders. Hmmm.

Because I had never seen the nonverbal section of the test, I pulled one from the file and gave it to myself. I didn't do as well as Paul.

I called his mother and asked if he were having trouble reading and if he had any proclivity for art. The teachers had told Paul's mother that he was having difficulty with symbolic material, but "he shows no talent for art. He *did* learn to play chess pretty well when he was four." Oh. We were dealing with a nine-year-old who had had been playing chess more than half his life. "Anything else along these lines?" I asked. "Yes," she laughed, "he always has figured out how to *win* at the videogames that I buy before I've even read the *instructions*." Oh.

We came to no firm conclusions that Friday afternoon, but I felt that Paul had a lot more going for him than the test showed. The teachers, it turned out, were keenly aware of his reading problems and over the summer had developed plans for bringing him along. They also said his spoken language was full of humor and creativity.

Tests don't measure humor and creativity. Tests test only a narrow range of human abilities. Unfortunately, they've taken on so much importance in deciding who is smart and who's not, that

> *Tests don't measure humor and creativity, just who is "smart."*

parents often feel their judgments are no match for those spewed out by the supercomputers of testing companies. The problems of the modern world are so complex, though, that we should encourage as much diversity of talent as possible in the hopes that decent solutions might occur to *someone.*

Even people in testing companies recognize the need for diversity. Way back in 1974, way before the current testing mania, Leo Munday and Jean Davis of the American College Testing Program wrote this:

> One of the undesirable by-products of testing practice has been the emphasis on academic talent with its accompanying indifference to other kinds of talent. Tests have fostered a narrow conception of ability and restricted the diversity of talent which might be brought to the attention of young people considering various professions. It is small wonder that some people have mistakenly interpreted test scores as measures of personal worth and have mistakenly assumed that academic talent as evidenced in schools is related in a major way to later adult accomplishment.[1]

Their 1974 research found that test scores were *not* related to later adult accomplishment, something overlooked in Nicholas Lemann's book about the SAT, *The Big Test.* As Herndon discovered, the test can only mean something if you never look at the kids themselves. In this test-mad society, that is a message that we should send home to every parent in the form of a refrigerator magnet that glows in the dark.

Note

1. Leo Munday and Jean Davis, "Varieties of Accomplishment After College: Perspectives on the Meaning of Academic Talent." Research Report #62: American College Testing Program, Iowa City, IA, 1974.

Long-Term Studies of Preschool
The Benefits Far Outweigh the Costs

GERALD W. BRACEY
Associate, High/Scope Educational Research
Foundation and Associate Professor, George Mason
University

ARTHUR STELLAR
Former President and CEO, High/Scope Educational
Research Foundation

The November 2001 issue of *Phi Delta Kappan* contained a special section providing a cross-national perspective on early childhood education and daycare. Daycare programs were described for England, Italy, and Sweden and contrasted with daycare here. The other countries, especially Sweden, have coherent, comprehensive programs based on a set of assumptions about the positive outcomes of early education.

In the United States, by contrast, there is a "nonsystem." Sharon Lynn Kagan and Linda Hallmark wrote, "In the U.S., not only has early childhood never been a national priority, but decades of episodic, on-again, off-again efforts have yielded a set of uncoordinated programs and insufficient investment in the infrastructure. Often, the most important components of high-quality education and care—financing, curriculum development, and teacher education—are neglected" (241).[1]

According to Kagan and Hallmark, the United States historically resisted having major government intrusion into education in the early years because of the perception that it signals failure on the part of the family. This produces a vicious circle: Parents resist government intervention in the education of young children on ideological grounds. The government doesn't produce high-quality daycare. Parents resist daycare on the grounds of low quality. Today, the keep-government-out-of-families ideology is still present in some quarters. David Salisbury of the Cato Institute put it this way: "The key to producing intelligent, healthy children does not lie in putting more of them in taxpayer-funded preschools. . . . Instead of forcing mothers into the workplace through heavy taxation, the government should reduce the tax burden on families and, thereby, allow child care to remain in the capable hands of parents."[2]

This is most unfortunate, as evidence is now strong that high-quality daycare produces long-term positive outcomes. Three studies of specific programs provide the evidence.

The "granddaddy" of these three studies is known as the High/Scope Perry Preschool Project.[3] In the mid 1960s, African-American children whose parents had applied to a preschool program in Ypsilanti, Michigan, were randomly assigned to receive the program or not. Those who tested the children, interviewed parents, or were the children's teachers once they reached school age did not know which group the children were in. Random assignment eliminates any systematic bias between the groups (although it cannot guarantee they will be the same). By keeping the information confidential, the experimenters prevented any kind of Pygmalion in the Classroom effects—effects from expectations deriving from knowing which children had been in preschool and which had not. Few preschool programs existed at the time, and children in the control group remained at home.

Parents of the children had completed 9.4 years of school on average. Only 20 percent had a high school diploma, compared with 33 percent of all African-American adults at the time of the study. Children attended preschool for a half-day for eight months. The first group of children, entering in 1962, received one year of the preschool program; later groups received two years. The program also included a weekly, ninety-minute home visit by project staff.

The vision of childhood underlying the High/Scope program was shaped by Piaget and other theorists who viewed children as active learners. Teachers asked questions that allowed children to generate conversations with them. Those who developed the program had isolated what they considered ten key categories of preschool experience important in developing children: creative representation, language and literacy, social relations and personal initiative, movement, music, classification, seriation (creating series and patterns), number, space, and time. Children participated in individual, small-group and large-group activities. The curriculum and instruction flowed from both constructivist and cognitive-developmental approaches.[4]

Teachers rarely assessed the children's specific knowledge. This approach stood in marked contrast to another preschool curriculum, Direct Instruction (DI). DI attempts to impart specific bits of knowledge through rapid-fire drills and highly programmed scripts.

A study of these "children" at age 40 is in progress. Other studies occurred when the children reached ages 19 and 27. At age 19, the preschoolers had higher graduation rates and were less likely to have been in special education. The graduation rate effect, though, was limited to females. The students also had higher scores on the Adult Performance Level Survey, a test from the American College Testing Program that simulates real-life problem situations.

By the time the two groups turned twenty-seven, 71 percent of the preschool group had a high school diploma or GED, compared with 54 percent of the control group. The preschoolers earned more, were more likely to own their own homes, and had longer and more stable marriages. Control group members were arrested twice as often, and five times as many of the control group (35 percent) had been arrested five or more times.

The second study is called the Abecedarian Project and has been run out of the University of North Carolina at Chapel Hill since 1972.[5] The study identified children at birth and provided them with full-day daycare from then until school entrance for fifty weeks a year. Adults would talk to the children, show them toys of pictures, offer them opportunities to react to sights and sounds in the environment. As the children grew, these adult–child interactions became more conceptually oriented and more skill oriented. For older preschoolers, they also became more group oriented. Some children continued in the program until age 8, while another group began to receive an enrichment program after they began school.

Although the children were randomly assigned, it is important to note that children in the "control" group were not without assistance. To reduce the chances that any differences might come from nutritional deficiencies affecting brain growth, the researcher supplied an enriched baby formula. Social work and crisis intervention services were also available to control group families. If the researchers' assessments indicated that the children were lagging developmentally, the families were referred to a relevant social agency. As a consequence of these policies and services, four of the control group children were moved to the head of the waiting list for what the researchers called "scarce slots in other quality community child centers."

In the decade since the Perry program began, early childhood education had become more prevalent, especially in university areas like Chapel Hill. Some of the control group families sent their kids to other preschool programs available in the area. It seems likely, therefore, that some children in the "control" group received benefits similar to those provided to the experimental group kids. These benefits would tend to reduce the differences seen between experimental and control groups.

Young adults who had taken part in the Abecedarian project completed more years of schooling (12.2 versus 11.6). As with the Perry program, this effect was largely due to the females in the study. More of the experimental group was still in school (42 percent versus 20 percent) and more had enrolled in four-year colleges (35.9 percent versus 13.7 percent). Forty-seven percent of the preschool group worked at skill jobs such as electrician, compared to 27 percent with the control group. The kids who had attended preschool were less likely to smoke or use marijuana, but no less likely to use alcohol or to indulge in binge drinking.

> *In all three longitudinal studies of children in pre-school, results indicate higher graduation rates and many other positive outcomes.*

The researchers administered reading and math tests at ages 8, 12, 15, and 21. Children in the program for eight years showed much better reading skills than those in the control. The effect sizes obtained ranged from 1.04 at age 8 to 0.79 at age 21. Effect sizes for math ranged from 0.64 at age 8 to 0.42 at age 21. Judgment must be used in interpreting effect sizes, but all researchers would likely consider these large except, perhaps, the 0.42 for math at age 21, which might be considered "medium."

For children who had terminated the program when they entered school, the reading effect sizes ran from 0.75 at age 8 to 0.28 at age 21. The math impact actually grew over time, being 0.27 at age 8 and 0.73 at age 21. Generally, it appears that children who continued with the Abecedarian program into the elementary grades were affected more than those who stopped at the end of preschool.

Children who received the school-only program showed smaller effect sizes. For reading, the effect size was 0.28 at age 8 and dwindled to 0.11 at age 21. Math again showed increased impact over time, being 0.11 at age 8 and 0.26 at age 21.

The third major long-term study of preschool payoffs is known as the Chicago Child-Parent Center Program (CPC).[6] It was a much larger study than the Perry or Abecedarian projects, but children were not randomly assigned to experimental and control groups. The CPC was also much more diffuse than the other projects, taking place in some twenty centers, and initially teachers had more latitude over what kinds of materials were incorporated. Later, all centers adopted a program developed through the Chicago Board of Education, emphasizing three major areas: body image and gross motor skills, perceptual-motor and arithmetic skills, and language.

As with the other projects, extensive parent involvement was emphasized. Project staff visited the homes, and parents often accompanied children on field trips. At age 21, children who had participated in the project had lower crime rates, higher high school completion rates, and fewer retentions in grade.

Quality Concerns

There is now some evidence to suggest that even diffuse, broad-scope programs such as Head Start produce increases in high school graduation rates and increases in college attendance.[7] It seems clear, though that high-quality programs are more effective. As laid out by Steve Barnett at Rutgers, to be high quality, programs should have the following characteristics:

■ Low child–teacher ratios

- Highly qualified and well-paid teachers
- Intellectually rich and broad curricula
- Parents engaged as active partners with the program
- Start dates at or before the child reaches age 3[8]

According to Kagan and Hallmark, many programs in the United States do not meet these criteria. Samuel Meisels of the Erikson Institute posits that the proposed "national reporting system" for Head Start will not bring such qualities to Head Start either.[9] Indeed, Meisels worries that the system might reduce the quality of Head Start and psychologically damage children.

Costs and Benefits

These preschool programs cost money, substantially more money than Head Start and even more than most preschools provided by private companies. The question arises as to whether the benefits from the programs are worth these costs. Cost–benefit analyses on all three conclude that they are.

A recent analysis of the Abecedarian project by Leonard Masse and W. Steven Barnett at Rutgers University concluded that the benefit–cost ratio for the program was 4:1.[10] That is, society received four dollars for every dollar invested. This is not as high as analyses for the Perry and Chicago projects. These latter yielded benefit–cost ratios on the order of 7:1. As noted, though, a number of children in the Abecedarian project had also participated in some preschool project, and this could have attenuated the ratio.

Are the benefits from these programs worth the cost? Analyses conclude they are.

Masse and Barnett estimated that children who took part in the program would earn $143,000 more over their lifetimes than those who did not. Their mothers would earn $133,000 more. The latter figure might initially surprise readers, but Masse and Barnett cite other studies, finding that given stable, continuous child care, mothers are able to effectively reallocate time that permits them to establish better, longer term, more productive relationships with employers.

Masse and Barnett also infer that the children of the children who participated in high-quality preschool programs will earn more as a consequence. Although it is difficult to quantify these projected earnings, they estimate a lifetime increase of $48,000 for the children of the participants. Although conjectural in the concrete, the logic is straightforward: The children who participate experience outcomes such as higher educational attainment, which are associated with higher earnings for future generations.

The cost–benefit analysts warn that these programs can be expensive. They estimated the Perry project at $9,200 per child per year, while the Abecedarian research came in at $13,900 (in constant 2002 dollars). This compares with $7,000 for Head Start. They worry that governments might experience "sticker shock" if they try to replicate these projects on a large-scale basis, but caution that "costs alone offer little guidance. The costs of a program must be compared against the benefits that the program generates. Benefit–cost ratios that are greater than 1 indicate that a program is worthy of consideration regardless of the absolute level of program costs" (14).

The programs described in this article all involve children living in poverty. Little if any research exists on long-term benefits for middle-class children. Masse and Barnett argue that if we limit the programs to children under age 5 and assume that 20 percent of those children live in poverty, the annual cost for quality preschool for those 20 percent would be $53 billion per year.

While the CED's report has been well received in both the business and education communities, states, facing their worst budget conditions since The Great Depression, have not responded.

Governments, however, appear to be looking at absolute costs. The Education Commission of the States reports that eight states have cut back on monies available for preschool in 2002–2003. Many writers mention that today, in early 2003, state government budgets are in their worst shape since World War II. Still, sentiment for universal preschool is growing. After reviewing the evidence on the impact of early childhood education, the Committee for Economic Development (CED)[11] led off a monograph thusly:

> The Committee for Economic Development calls on the federal and state governments to undertake a new national compact to

make early education available to all children age 3 and over. To ensure that all children have the opportunity to enter school ready to learn, the nation needs to reform its current, haphazard, piecemeal and underfunded approach to early learning by linking programs and providers to coherent state-based systems. The goal should be universal access to free, high-quality prekindergarten classes, offered by a variety of providers for all children whose parents want them to participate. (1)

Such a program, at least to the authors, makes much more sense than a program that tests all children in grades 3 through 8 in reading, math, and science. Alas, Chris Dreibelbis at the CED reports that while the CED's monograph has been well received in both the education and business communities, there is little movement that might make the proposal a reality.[12]

Notes

1. Sharon L. Kagan and Linda G. Hallmark, "Early Child and Education Policies in Sweden: Implications for the United States." *Phi Delta Kappan,* November 2001, pp. 237–245.

2. David Salisbury, "Preschool Is Overhyped." *USA Today,* September 18, 2002.

3. John R. Berrueta-Clement, Lawrence J. Schweinhart, W. Steven Barnett, Ann S. Epstein, and David P. Weikart, *Changed Lives: The Effects of the Perry Preschool Program on Youths Through Age 19.* Ypsilanti, MI: High/Scope Press, 1984. Also see Lawrence J. Schweinhart, Helen V. Barnes, and David P. Weikart, *Significant Benefits: The High/Scope Perry Preschool Student Through Age 27.* Ypsilanti, MI: High/Scope Press, 1993.

4. M. Hohmann and David P. Weikart, *Educating Young Children: Active Learning Practices for Preschool and Child Care Programs.* Ypsilanti, MI: High/Scope Press, 1995.

5. Frances A. Campbell, Craig T. Ramey, Elizabeth P. Pungello, Joseph Sparling, and Shari Miller-Johnson, "Early Childhood Education: Young Adult Outcomes for the Abecedarian Project." *Applied Developmental Science,* 2002, 6, pp. 42–57. Frances A. Campbell, Elizabeth P. Pungello, Shari Miller-Johnson, Margaret Burchinal, and Craig T. Ramey, "The Development of Cognitive and Academic Abilities: Growth Curves from an Early Childhood Experiment."

Developmental Psychology, 2001, *37,* pp. 231–42.

6. Arthur J. Reynolds, Judy A. Temple, Dylan L. Robertson, and Emily A. Mann, "Age 21 Benefit-Cost Analysis of the Chicago Child-Parent Center Program." Paper presented to the Society for Prevention Research, Madison, WI, May 21 to June 2, 2001. See also Arthur J. Reynolds, Judy A. Temple, Dylan L. Robertson, and Emily A. Mann, "Long-Term Effects of an Early Childhood Intervention on Educational Achievement and Juvenile Arrest." *Journal of the American Medical Association,* May 9, 2001.

7. Eliana Garces, Duncan Thomas, and Janet Currie, "Longer Terms Effects of Head Start." National Bureau of Economic Research, Working Paper 8054, December 2000. Available at www.nber.org/papers/w8054. See also Janet Currie and Duncan Thomas, "School Quality and the Longer-Term Effects of Head Start." *Journal of Human Resources,* Fall 2000, pp. 755–74.

8. W. Steven Barnett, "Early Childhood Education." In *School Reform Proposals: The Research Evidence,* ed. Alex Molnar. Greenwich, CT: IAP Information Age Publishing, 2002. Also accessible at www.asu.edu/educ/epsl (Click on Education Policy Research Unit, then under Archives, click on Research and Writing.)

9. Samuel J. Meisels, "Can Head Start Pass the Test?" *Education Week,* March 19, 2003, p. 44.

10. Leonard N. Masse and W. Steven Barnett, *Benefit Cost Analysis of the Abecedarian Early Childhood Intervention Project.* New Brunswick, NJ: National Institute for Early Childhood Research, Rutgers University, 2002.

11. Committee for Economic Development, *Preschool for All: Investing in a Productive and Just Society.* New York: Author, 2002.

12. Personal communication, February 3, 2003.